I0024296

George Weir

In the Court of Error and Appeal for Upper Canada

Weir v. Mathieson, case on appeal from a decree of the Court of Chancery, the

Reverend Alexander Mathieson and others, appellants, and the Reverend George

Weir and others, respondents

George Weir

In the Court of Error and Appeal for Upper Canada
Weir v. Mathieson, case on appeal from a decree of the Court of Chancery, the Reverend Alexander Mathieson and others, appellants, and the Reverend George Weir and others, respondents

ISBN/EAN: 9783337373474

Printed in Europe, USA, Canada, Australia, Japan

Cover: Foto ©Suzi / pixelio.de

More available books at **www.hansebooks.com**

IN THE

Court of Error and Appeal

FOR UPPER CANADA.

WEIR v. MATHIESON.

CASE ON APPEAL FROM A DECREE OF THE COURT OF CHANCERY.

THE REVEREND ALEXANDER MATHIESON AND OTHERS,

APPELLANTS ;

AND

THE REVEREND GEORGE WEIR AND OTHERS,

RESPONDENTS.

MACLENNAN, GRAHAME AND HENDERSON,

Solicitors for Appellants ;

CROOKS, KINGSMILL AND CATTANACH,

Solicitors for Respondents.

TORONTO:
PRINTED AT THE GLOBE STEAM JOB PRESS, 26 & 28 KING STREET EAST.
1865.

INDEX.

In the Court of Error and Appeal.

AN APPEAL FROM THE COURT OF CHANCERY.

Between THE REVEREND GEORGE WEIR,

Plaintiff;

AND

THE REVEREND ALEXANDER MATHIESON, THE REVEREND
HUGH URQUHART, THE REVEREND ALEXANDER SPENCE,
THE REVEREND JOHN McMORINE, THE REVEREND WILLIAM
MAXWELL INGLIS, THE REVEREND JAMES WILLIAMSON,
THE REVEREND DUNCAN MORRISON, THE REVEREND GEORGE
BELL, THE HONOURABLE JOHN HAMILTON, JOHN PATON,
GEORGE DAVIDSON, GEORGE NEILSON, JOHN CAMERON,
ALEXANDER McLEAN, HUGH ALLAN, ALEXANDER MORRIS,
GEORGE MALLOCH, ALEXANDER LOGIE, THE REVEREND
JOHN COOK, D.D., THE REVEREND JAMES C. MUIR, D.D., THE
REVEREND JOHN BARCLAY, D.D., JOHN THOMPSON, JOHN
GREENSHIELDS, EDWARD MALLOCH, ANDREW DRUMMOND,
AND THE HONOURABLE ARCHIBALD McLEAN, AND QUEEN'S
COLLEGE AT KINGSTON.

Defendants.

The appeal of the above-named Defendants, The Reverend Alexander Mathieson, The Reverend Hugh Urquhart, The Reverend Alexander Spence, The Reverend Duncan Morrison, The Reverend George Bell, The Honourable John Hamilton, John Paton, George Davidson, George Neilson, John Cameron, Alexander McLean, Hugh Allan, Alexander Morris, Alexander Logie, The Reverend James C. Muir, The Reverend John Barclay, Andrew Drummond, The Honourable Archibald McLean, and Queen's College at Kingston.

The Plaintiff's Bill of Complaint.

Filed 12th March, 1861.

Amended 17th September, 1861, under order of even date

NOTE.—The amended parts are printed in italics.

CITY OF KINGSTON.

TO THE HONORABLE THE JUDGES OF THE COURT OF CHANCERY.

The Bill of Complaint of the Reverend George Weir, of the City of Kingston, Master of Arts, Professor of Classical Literature in the University of Queen's College at Kingston,

Showeth as follows:

1. By Royal Letters Patent issued on the sixteenth day of October, one thousand eight hun-

dred and forty-two, after reciting amongst other things that the establishment of a College in the Province of Upper Canada, in connection with the Church of Scotland, for the education of youth in the principles of the Christian Religion, and for their instruction in the various branches of Science and Literature, would greatly conduce to the welfare of the said Province, Her Majesty was pleased to grant, constitute, declare and appoint certain persons therein particularly named, being ministers of the Presbyterian Church of Canada, in connection with the Church of Scotland, or members of such Church, to be a body corporate by the name of " Queen's College at Kingston," with perpetual succession as a College with the style and privileges of a University, for the education and instruction of youth and students in arts and faculties, with capacity to receive and hold lands and hereditaments to the amount of fifteen thousand pounds sterling, in annual value and personal property of every nature, and to alienate such lands, hereditaments, and personal property.

2. The said Letters Patent further declared that, for the better execution of the purposes set forth in the said Letters Patent, and for the more regular government of the said Corporation, that such Corporation should for ever have twenty-seven Trustees, such Trustees to be nominated and appointed as in the said Letters mentioned, and amongst other powers thereby conferred on the said Trustees, the said Letters Patent declared that they should for ever have full power and authority to elect and appoint for the said College, a Principal, and such Professor or Professors, Master or Masters, Tutor or Tutors, and such other Officer or Officers as to the said Trustees should seem meet ; and further " that if any complaint respecting the conduct of the Principal, " or any Professor, Master, Tutor, or other Officer of the said College, be at any time made to the " Board of Trustees, they may institute an enquiry, and in the event of any impropriety of con- " duct being duly proved, they shall admonish, reprove, suspend or remove the person offending, " as to them may seem good, Provided always that the grounds of such admonition, reproof, " suspension or removal be recorded at length in the books of the said Board ;" and further, that the said Trustees should have power to make Statutes and Rules concerning, amongst other things, the good government of the said College, the number, residence, and duties of the professors thereof, the management of the revenues and property of the said College, the salaries, stipends, provisions and emoluments of and for the Professors thereof, provided that such Statutes and Rules should not be repugnant to the said Letters Patent, or to the Laws and Statutes of Upper Canada ; and further, that five of the said Trustees lawfully convened as was thereinafter directed, should be a quorum for the despatch of all business except for disposal and purchase of real estate, or for the choice or removal of the Principal or Professors, for any of which purposes there should be a meeting of at least thirteen Trustees ; and further, that the said Trustees should have power to meet at Kingston, aforesaid, or at such other place as they should fix for that purpose upon their own adjournment, and likewise so often as they should be summoned by the Chairman, or in his absence, by the Senior Trustee, provided however, that the Chairman or Senior Trustee should not summon a meeting of the Trustees unless required so to do by a notice in writing from three members of the Board, and provided also that due notice of the time and place of the said meeting to be given in one or more of the public newspapers of the Province of Upper and Lower Canada, at least thirty days before such meeting, and that every member of the Board of Trustees, resident within the said Province, should be notified in writing by the Secretary to the Corporation, of the time and place of such meeting ; and in and by the said Letters Patent, the Principal of the said College, and all the Professors thereof, were constituted "The College Senate," for the exercise of academical superintendence and discipline over the students and all other persons resident within the same.

3. In the year one thousand eight hundred and fifty-three, the Reverend John Cook, Doctor of Divinity, and the first Principal of the said College, was directed by the Board of Trustees to proceed to Scotland and procure Professors for the said University, and, the Plaintiff who was then filling the permanent office of Rector of the Grammar School of Banff, in Scotland, aforesaid, was desired by Dr. Cook to accept the Professorship of Classical Literature in the University of Queen's College at Kingston, and in September, one thousand eight hundred and fifty-three, the Plaintiff still being in Scotland, aforesaid, accepted such office, the salary or yearly emoluments thereof being fixed at the sum of Three Hundred and Fifty Pounds.

4. In October, one thousand eight hundred and fifty-three, the Plaintiff entered upon the discharge of the duties of his said Professorship, and was then duly confirmed by the Board of Trustees of the said College, in the said office of Professor of Classical Literature, and from such appointment and confirmation in office by the said Trustees, the Plaintiff hath continued to faithfully perform and discharge the duties of his said Professorship thence until recently ; and in the month of February, one thousand eight hundred and sixty-four, he has been hindered and prevented in the discharge of such duties by the wrongful, improper and illegal acts hereinafter mentioned.

5. On the eighteenth day of February, one thousand eight hundred and sixty-four, the Board of Trustees of the said College passed the following resolution :—" Resolved, That from " the facts which have come to the knowledge of the Trustees, and the present alarming state of the " College, the Trustees deem it necessary, in the interest of the College, to remove Professor Weir " from the office of Professor of Classics and Secretary to the Senatus, and in the exercise of " their power to remove at discretion, they hereby do remove him from these offices accordingly " forthwith, and that the Treasurer do pay to him his salary in full to the end of the present " session, and for six months thereafter in advance in lieu of notice, and that the Secretary be " instructed to communicate this resolution to Mr. Weir."

6. On this resolution being communicated to the Plaintiff, the Plaintiff refused to recognize its validity or to acquiesce therein in anywise, and notwithstanding such resolution, the Plaintiff endeavoured to perform, and would have performed, and has always been ready and willing to perform the duties of his Professorship, but the Board of Trustees have excluded and still continue to exclude him from the said College, and refuse to permit him in any manner to discharge his said office of Professor of Classics, and the Board of Trustees refuse to allow to the Plaintiff the privileges and emoluments appertaining to his said office, and are endeavouring to enforce the aforesaid resolution of the Eighteenth day of February, one thousand eight hundred and sixty-four.

7. The Plaintiff shews that by means of gifts, donations and bequests from a large number of individual members of the Church of Scotland, and others, and from other sources the said College is possessed of, and interested in divers large and valuable property and effects, and of and from the annual income arising from such property, and from any grant of moneys from the Legislature the Board of Trustees of the said College may and discharge the salaries of the Professors of the said College and the other expenses of the said College, and such properties and moneys are expressly vested in, and held by, such Trustees in Trust to pay and apply the same in discharge of such salaries and expenses, in accordance with and under and subject to the declarations, provisions, powers and authorities in the said Letters Patent contained.

6

7 b. The Plaintiff shews that the Royal Charter aforesaid was granted by Her Majesty to the intent that the members of the Church of Scotland in Canada might have and enjoy a University and College, with similar powers and privileges, and upon the model of the University of Edinburgh, and the said Royal Charter was and is based and founded upon this consideration, and Her Majesty in and by the said Royal Charter, wherein she is pleased to make provision for the appointment and removal of Professors in the said College, had in view Professors enjoying similar office and fulfilling similar duties to the Professors in the University of Edinburgh, and that similar usages and customs should apply to and be associated with such Professorship, and that the nature of such office and employment should be similar in the said two Universities. In the University of Edinburgh the tenure of the office of a Professor is *ad vitam aut culpam*, that is during the life of the Incumbent, unless removed for impropriety of conduct, and such the Plaintiff submits under the Royal Charter aforesaid is the tenure of the aforesaid Professorship, held by the Plaintiff in Queen's College, and the Plaintiff further states that such was the condition under which the Plaintiff accepted his said appointment, and that the said Trustees have also further so regarded the said office of Professor, and declarations and entries to that effect appear on the records of their proceedings.

8. The Plaintiff states that the aforesaid resolution of the Eighteenth day of February, one thousand eight hundred and sixty-four, was passed by the Board of Trustees without the Plaintiff being present, without his being notified or requested to appear before such Board, without his being notified of any charge or complaint, without his being summoned before the Board to answer any charge or complaint, without any charge or complaint being preferred against him, and without the Board having called upon the Plaintiff to make any defence, and without having asked from him any explanation whatever.

9. Since the Board passed the aforesaid resolution, the Plaintiff hath been informed and now shews to this Honourable Court that the Board, in passing such resolution, acted upon an *ex parte* statement of the Reverend William Leitch, the now Principal of the said College, and one of the Defendants hereto, in which he alleged, in effect, that the Plaintiff had conceived malice against him, and that he judged that such existed from the part taken by the Plaintiff on the occasion of the presentation of the address of the Medical Faculty of the said College to Dr. Lawson upon his resignation of his Professorship in such Faculty; that the Plaintiff had been the cause of breaking up the Grammar School; that the Plaintiff had called a meeting of the Senatus, although wished by the Defendant, Leitch, not to do so; that the Plaintiff had complained of certain Statutes of the Board as illegal, and that the Plaintiff had written a letter to a newspaper in Kingston, called "The British Whig," as to the tenure of the office held by the Plaintiff in Scotland before accepting the said Professorship of Classics; but the Plaintiff is unable to set forth more specifically the allegations contained in the said statement, inasmuch as such statement was only read to the Board by one of the said Trustees at the request and on behalf of the Defendant, Leitch, and so soon as read returned to the said Leitch, and such statement was not entered or allowed to be entered in the minutes or proceedings of the said Board, and the said Board, immediately after hearing such statement read, and without having had or called for any proof or evidence of the allegations thereby made, assumed to remove the Plaintiff from his aforesaid office.

10. At a meeting of the Trustees of the said College, held at Kingston, aforesaid, on the twenty-sixth day of January, one thousand eight hundred and sixty-three, whereat there were

7

present the Honourable John Hamilton, the Reverend Dr. Leitch, the Reverend Dr. Williamson, the Reverend Dr. Urquhart, the Reverend Duncan Morrison, Alexander McLean, Hugh Allan, Alexander Morris, John Paton, and Andrew Drummond, a Code or set of Statutes, Rules and Ordinances were assumed to be enacted, and amongst such Statutes, Rules and Ordinances, the said Board of Trustees assumed to enact the following (with others), that is to say :—

" 10. All Officers shall be appointed shall have their duties prescribed by and shall hold
" office only during the pleasure of the Trustees, except in cases where a special agreement may
" have been or may be made, and shall be entitled to such salaries or emoluments as may be
" from time to time . greed on."

" 14. The Trustees may, on their own motion, and without complaint being made, deal with
" the Principal, Professors, Janitors, or any other officer, when they see cause. In such case, it
" shall not be necessary that the grounds of censure, suspension or removal be recorded, the
" recording of the grounds being warranted only in the case of a judicial process, in which a
" complainant acts as prosecutor. An officer being removed shall be entitled to claim salary
" only up to the date of removal."

" 27. He (that is the Principal) shall sign all minutes of meeting of College, Senate and Sena-
" tus, and should any meeting be held in his absence, the decisions of the meetings shall not be
" valid till the minutes have received his signature or approval."

11. The meeting of the said Trustees of the twenty-sixth day of January, one thousand eight hundred and sixty-three, mentioned in the last preceding paragraph, was an illegal meeting. and not convened according to the requirements of the Royal Charter, inasmuch as many of the said Trustees were not summoned or notified to attend, and some of them were only notified by telegraph two or three days before such meeting, and the said Statutes were passed at the said meeting without the knowledge of the major part of the said Trustees, and in their absence the said Statutes had been drawn up previously to such meeting by the Reverend Dr. Leitch, without any consultation or communication with the College, Senate, or any of the Professors of the said College, and the said Statutes were read and passed at the same meeti. ; in which they were introduced, and no opportunity was afforded for any consideration or discussion of them by the major part of the said Trustees. The Trustees who were present at such meeting and passed the said Statutes had been prepared beforehand by the Reverend Dr. Leitch, and were pledged by him to the passing of the said Statutes at some private meeting, and the said Statutes were enacted without that deliberation which the said Trustees, in the bona fide exercise of their duties, should otherwise have given to them.

12. The Plaintiff shews that in many respects the Statutes so enacted, as aforesaid, were and are illegal, and contrary to the Royal Charter, and especially the Statutes 10, 14 and 27, set forth in the tenth paragraph of this Bill. Statute 10 is contrary to the Charter and illegal, inasmuch as it assumes to make the tenure of all offices in the said College to be at the pleasure of the said Trustees. Statute 14 is also illegal and contrary to the Charter, inasmuch as it assumes to confer on the said Trustees a power on their own mere motion, and without any cause assigned of removing any of the Professors or Officers of the said College ; and Statute 27 assumes to give to the Principal a veto on all proceedings of the College Senate, which is not conferred or con-templated by the said Charter.

2

13. The Plaintiff, and other Professors in the said College, so soon as they became aware of the passing of the said Statutes in the month of February, one thousand eight hundred and sixty-three, objected to and protested against the said Statutes, upon the grounds hereinbefore stated, and such objections have been continued up to the present time, and in consequence of such objections and protest, the said Trustees appointed a Committee to consider and report upon such Statutes, which Committee has not, however, made any report thereon.

14. The passing of the said Statutes under the circumstances hereinbefore stated, and the general tendency thereof being to confer on the Reverend Dr. Leitch, as the Principal, of the absolute control of the other Professors in the said College, and to make the tenure of their office or offices to depend upon his mere pleasure, caused great dissatisfaction and discontent amongst the Professors, Students, and others interested in the said College, and in consequence of such statutes Dr. Lawson, one of the Professors in the said College, in September, one thousand eight hundred and sixty-three, resigned his Professorship, and this further increased the prevailing discontent in the said College.

15. The alarming state of the College referred to in the Resolution of the eighteenth day of February, one thousand eight hundred and sixty-four, was solely caused by these obnoxious statutes, and by the refusal of the Trustees to pay any regard to the respectful remonstrances made to them with respect thereto, and the Plaintiff did not cause or originate such a state of things, and the alleged complaint against the Plaintiff, in that behalf is entirely unfounded.

16. The Plaintiff shews that the meeting of the said Trustees, held on the ninth and tenth days of February, one thousand eight hundred and sixty-four, was illegal and contrary to the Charter of the said College, and was not duly summoned or convened. The said meeting professed to be an adjourned meeting from the third day of February, one thousand eight hundred and sixty-four, on which occasion there were only three of the said Trustees present, and these had no power to adjourn the said meeting, and no notice was given to the different Trustees of the said meeting of the ninth day of February, one thousand eight hundred and sixty-four, in the manner prescribed by the said Charter.

17. The Plaintiff shews that before the said meeting of the ninth day of February, one thousand eight hundred and sixty-four, took place, the major part of the said Trustees had been privately and secretly influenced, and were prejudiced against him by the Reverend Dr. Leitch, and having been so previously influenced and prejudiced against the Plaintiff, the major part of the said Trustees were prepared at such meeting to remove the Plaintiff from his said office, without giving the Plaintiff any opportunity of being heard or of justifying himself.

18. At such meeting all of the Defendants hereto, excepting the Reverend Dr. Leitch, the Reverend John Cook, the Reverend James C. Muir, the Reverend John Barclay, John Thompson, John Greenshields, Edward Malloch, Andrew Drummond, and the Hon. Archibald McLean, were present, and of such as were present, George Malloch and the Reverend Dr. Williamson voted against the removal of the Plaintiff, and the Reverend Messrs. MacMorine and Inglis declined to vote, whilst all the others voted for the passing of the aforesaid Resolution of the tenth day of February, one thousand eight hundred and sixty-four.

19. The Plaintiff further shews that such Resolution was prepared and passed by the said

Trustees in consequence of the influence of the Reverend Dr. Leitch upon them, and in so influencing the said Trustees the Reverend Dr. Leitch was actuated by feelings of resentment against the Plaintiff, in consequence of the objections made by him, with other Professors, to the aforesaid Statutes, and on account of the independence of the Plaintiff's character, and from his not submitting, in the College, Senate, or otherwise, to the dictation of the Reverend Dr. Leitch.

20. The Plaintiff further shews that the said Trustees were not justified by any of the statements made by the Reverend Dr. Leitch to the said Trustees, even if the same were true, in the passing of the aforesaid resolution, and that such Resolution was and is the result of party and prejudiced feeling, and not of consideration for what is to the advantage and benefit of the said College.

21. The Plaintiff shews that the Defendants threaten and intend to discontinue the payment of the Plaintiff's said salary and emolument attached to his said office of Professor, and also to resist and prevent him in his endeavor to discharge and perform the duties thereof.

22. *The Plaintiff shews that since the filing of this Bill the Defendants, on the thirtieth day of May last, assumed to pass the two Resolutions set forth in the supplemental answer of the said Defendants, but the Plaintiff charges that the meeting of the said Trustees, at which such resolutions were passed, was illegally and improperly convened and held, and that the proper notices required by the Charter in that behalf were not previously given, or, if given, not within the time required by the said Charter.*

23. *The Plaintiff further charges that the Defendants did not summon or call upon the Plaintiff to appear at such last mentioned meeting, and that the resolutions passed at the said meeting were come to without any complaint made against the Plaintiff, or any proof or evidence thereupon and without discussion and deliberation by the said Trustees, and were passed merely for the purpose of giving additional colour and pretended confirmation to the void and illegal acts complained of in his aforesaid Bill.*

The Plaintiff under the circumstances hereinbefore stated therefore prays as follows :—

1. That it be declared that the aforesaid Resolutions of the Eighteenth day of February, one thousand eight hundred and sixty-four, was and is illegal and void, upon the ground that the meeting at which the same was passed was not duly held, and upon the ground that there was no complaint made against the Plaintiff, and no impropriety of conduct on his part proved.

2. That it may be declared that the aforesaid Resolution was and is a Breach of Trust and contrary to the duties reposed by the Royal Charter in the said Trustees, inasmuch as such resolution was passed without proper deliberation and consideration, and under the influence of prejudiced statements made without cause against the Plaintiff.

3. That it may be declared that the Statutes in the tenth paragraph of the said Bill particularly set forth in so far as they would afford any colour and ground for such resolution may be declared to be illegal and void upon the grounds hereinbefore set forth.

4. That it may be declared that the Plaintiff is entitled to hold and enjoy his said office of Professor of Classical Literature in the College aforesaid until duly removed or suspended therefrom for impropriety of conduct, duly proved, as contemplated by the Royal Charter aforesaid.

5. That the said Resolution may be cancelled, and the said Trustees restrained by the Order and Injunction of this Honorable Court, to be issued for that purpose, from in any wise interfering with or impeding the Plaintiff in the discharge and performance of the duties of his said office, and from withholding from him the Salary and Emoluments payable in respect thereof.

6. That all the Trustees, Defendants hereto, who voted for the aforesaid Resolution, and the Defendant, the Reverend William Leitch, may be ordered to pay the costs of this suit.

7. That the Plaintiff may have such further and other relief in the premises as the circumstances of this case may require.

(Signed)   ADAM CROOKS.

THE ANSWER OF THE REVEREND ALEXANDER MATHIESON, THE REVEREND HUGH URQUHART, THE REVEREND ALEXANDER SPENCE, THE REVEREND DUNCAN MORRISON, THE REVEREND GEORGE BELL, THE HONOURABLE JOHN HAMILTON, JOHN PATON, GEORGE DAVIDSON, GEORGE NEILSON, JOHN CAMERON, ALEXANDER McLEAN, HUGH ALLAN, ALEXANDER MORRIS, AND ALEXANDER LOGIE, FOURTEEN OF THE DEFENDANTS TO THE BILL OF COMPLAINT OF THE REVEREND GEORGE WEIR, COMPLAINANT.

Filed 10th May, 1854.

1. We submit that the Board of Trustees of the said Institution has power to appoint the Professors as well as the Masters, Tutors and Officers of the Institution for such term as the Board from time to time thinks proper.

2. We believe that many Professorships in the Colleges of the United Kingdom, and of the Continent of Europe, and also in Canada, and elsewhere in America, were not formerly, and many are not now held for life.

3. The usages and customs of the University of Edinburgh vary in many important respects from the provisions relating to Queen's College at Kingston, contained in the Royal Charter of that Institution, and we submit that in points not provided for by the said charter, the usages and customs of the Edinburgh University are not binding, and were not intended to be binding on Queen's College aforesaid.

4. The Plaintiff was not appointed Professor for life.

5. To the best of our knowledge, information and belief, he did not, as he alleges, accept the office on condition that the appointment should be for life, and the Trustees did not so regard it, and so far as we are aware, declarations and entries to that effect do not appear in the records of their proceedings.

6. The authority of the Reverend Dr. Cook, to which the Plaintiff refers, was contained in a resolution passed by the Board of Trustees at an adjourned meeting held on the fifteenth day of July, one thousand eight hundred and fifty-two. This resolution was as follows:

"That the committee of nomination, previously appointed, be discharged, and that the act-"ing Committee of the Colonial Committee, with the Reverend Dr. Mathieson, and the Reverend "Dr. Cook, or whichever of them may be in Scotland, be requested, and are hereby authorized "to seek out and recommend for appointment by the Board, Professors to fill the vacancies now "existing in the College."

7. The part which was taken by Dr. Cook in nominating the Plaintiff, appears from the following extract from the minutes of the Board, dated twentieth July, one thousand eight hundred and fifty-three :

3

" Dr. Cook gave a verbal report of his proceedings in Scotland in regard to the appointment
" of Professors, laid on the table minutes of the General Assembly's Colonial Committee on that
" subject, as also testimonials in favour of Mr. Weir and Mr. Geddes, and further expressed in
" strong terms, the favourable opinion entertained of the Reverend Mr. Milroy by Dr. Fleming,
" Professor of Moral Philosophy in the University of Glasgow."

8. The following resolution was thereupon submitted to the Board and passed :

" Moved by the Reverend James George, seconded by the Reverend Alexander Spence, and
" resolved, That Dr. Cook be authorized to write to Professor Menzies, in name of the Board, re-
" questing him to nominate Mr. Weir or Mr. Geddes to the Classical chair in this University, or
" failing them, such other person as he thinks qualified."

9. After the said Plaintiff had been nominated under the authority of these resolutions, and
on the eight day of June, one thousand eight hundred and fifty-four, the Trustees passed the
following resolution :

" That the appointment of Professor Weir be approved of and confirmed from the period of
his arrival in Kingston."

10. We believe that the appointment of the said Complainant, whether legal or not, rests
on these two resolutions, and we believe that the Office of Rector of the Grammar School at
Banff, was not, and is not, a permanent office as the Bill alleges, and was not held as such by
the Plaintiff.

11. We submit that the provisions of the said Letters Patent respecting the trial of complaints made to the Board, do not take away any discretionary power which the Trustees would
otherwise have, but are only obligatory where no such discretionary power exists.

12. We submit that the Board had discretionary power to dispense with the services of the
Plaintiff as Professor, just as the Board had like power to remove any Officer of the College,
subject to his receiving any payment on account of his salary, which the law under the circumstances might entitle him to, and that the Trustees having dispensed with the Plaintiff's services
in the exercise of their discretion, their act, or its motives, cannot be questioned by the Plaintiff
in this suit.

13. But we positively and distinctly deny that he was removed through such influence or
prejudice, or from such motives or feelings, or for such objects as the Bill alleges.

14. On the contrary, his removal was after a full discussion by the Board on the ninth and
tenth days of February last, and from a conviction that the conduct of the Plaintiff had rendered
his removal absolutely necessary for the best interests of the College. We further say, that
many of the facts and circumstances which shewed the necessity for his removal were within the
personal knowledge of the Trustees themselves.

15. The alarming state of the College referred to in the resolution respecting the Plaintiff's

removal, passed on the tenth and eighteenth day of February last, and the Plaintiff's share in producing such alarming state of the College, existed in part before the twenty-sixth day of January, one thousand eight hundred and sixty-three, and the necessity for the Statutes, Rules and Ordinances, passed on that day, partly arose from such condition of the Institution.

16. We submit that the Plaintiff has no right to raise any question as to the technical irregularity of the Meeting of the Board at which he was removed, his removal at discretion being, as we submit, within the power of the Board, and his removal, as the Plaintiff well knows, being the wish, and having the approbation of the great majority of the Trustees, including both those who were present at the said Meeting, and those who happened to be absent therefrom.

17. But we further submit, that the Meeting was regular, that a quorum was not necessary, and has never since the Board was first constituted been considered to be necessary for a motion of adjournment to a future day; that a different rule would be extremely inconvenient in a practice, prejudicial to the proper management of the affairs of the University, and attended with no corresponding advantage; that Meetings of the Board at which no quorum was present, have often been adjourned by those present to a future day specified day; that this practice has been accepted, and recognized, and acted on by the Trustees since the establishment of the University; that the Adjourned Meetings have in such cases taken place without objection; that by this means all the Trustees in effect vested in the Trustees who might happen to be present at any Meeting regularly called, the power of adjourning the same to a future specified day, and that in such case such adjourned Meeting was, and is in effect, a continuation of the original Meeting; that the Meeting at which the resolutions of the fifteenth July, one thousand eight hundred and fifty-two, and eighth June, one thousand eight hundred and fifty-four, were passed relative to the Plaintiff's appointment, were adjourned Meetings of this kind of which the notices specified in the Statute were not given; that timely notice of the adjourned meeting at which the Plaintiff was removed, was given to every Trustee by a letter addressed to him by the Secretary and otherwise.

18. We further say, that we do not believe that in the part the Reverend Principal took in the removal of the Plaintiff, and which is greatly misrepresented in the said Bill, the Principal was actuated by a feeling of resentment against the said Plaintiff, arising either from such reasons as the Bill states, or any other reasons; but, on the contrary, we believe that the Reverend Principal was actuated therein by a sense of duty to the Institution over which he presided, and by no wrong whatever. He was not present at the Meetings of the ninth and tenth February, being at the time, and having been for several weeks, seriously and dangerously ill as he still is.

19. We further submit that the said Plaintiff has no right to impeach the legality of the Statutes, Rules and Ordinances of the Twenty-sixth day of January, One thousand eight hundred and sixty-three, or the regularity of the meeting of the Board at which they were passed.

20. But we further submit that the said Statutes, Rules and Ordinances were legal, and that the meeting at which they were adopted was a legal meeting.

21. Such meeting was in fact an adjourned meeting, and the meeting of which it was an adjournment was a regular meeting which had been called in the manner prescribed in the Letters Patent, and a timely notice of the adjourned meeting was sent, we are informed and believe, to all the Trustees.

22. The said Statutes, Rules and Ordinances were not passed without due consideration and discussion, and the same had the approbation of most of the Trustees who were absent from the meeting as well as those who were present, and accordingly the same have been acquiesced in ever since.

23. We further submit that the said University was founded by Royal Charter, as stated in the first paragraph of the Plaintiff's Bill, and, therefore, that Her Majesty the Queen is the Visitor of the said University, and the Plaintiff's only remedy is by petition to Her Majesty.

24. We humbly submit that the Plaintiff is not entitled to any part of the relief prayed by the said Bill, on the ground that the Plaintiff should have appealed to Her Majesty the Queen as Visitor. And, further, that he is not entitled to the relief prayed on his own showing, or on the facts as they really are, and we claim the same benefit, of any defence appearing on the said Bill, as if we had demurred thereto, and we pray to be hence dismissed with costs.

O. MOWAT.

THE ANSWER OF THE DEFENDANTS THE REVEREND JOHN BARCLAY, HONORABLE ARCHIBALD McLEAN, REVEREND JAMES C. MUIR, AND ANDREW DRUMMOND.

Filed 6th May, 1861.

1. We say that the imputations in the said Bill contained against the Reverend Principal Leitch and the Trustees who voted for the removal of the Plaintiff, and for the Statutes, Rules, and Ordinances mentioned in the Bill, are, in our judgment, entirely unfounded and unjustifiable.

2. We believe that the Plaintiff did not hold his office for life, but was liable to removal at the discretion of the Trustees, and we believe that that discretion was exercised in good faith and from a conviction on the part of the Trustees who voted for the Plaintiff's removal, that his course of conduct had rendered his removal indispensable.

3. We submit that the Plaintiff, in and by his said Bill, does not show himself to be entitled to any equity, and we crave the same benefit of this defence as if we had demurred to the said Bill.

4. We further submit that not having been present at any of the meetings, the proceedings of which the Plaintiff complains of, we were unnecessary parties to the said Bill, and we pray that the same may be dismissed against us with costs.

THE ANSWER OF THE DEFENDANTS QUEEN'S COLLEGE AT KINGSTON.

Filed 10th May, 1861.

1. The Plaintiff's course of conduct persisted in, in spite of admonition, warning and advice, rendered his removal necessary for the best interests of the College.

2. We submit that the Board of Trustees had the power of removing the Plaintiff, and in the exercise of their power did duly remove him from his office.

3. We further submit that the Statutes, Rules and Ordinances referred to in the Bill, were such as the Board had power to adopt, and that they were legally and duly passed, and that whether they were or not, the Plaintiff has no right to impeach them in this suit.

4. We crave leave to refer to the joint and several answer of the Reverend Alexander Mathieson and others to the said Bill, as part of the answers of this Corporation, and we rely on the several grounds of defence therein set up to the Plaintiff's Bill.

5. We submit that the Plaintiff, in and by his said Bill, does not show himself to be entitled to any relief in equity, and we crave the same benefit of this defence as if we had demurred to the said Bill.

THE SUPPLEMENTARY ANSWER OF QUEEN'S COLLEGE AT KINGSTON.

DATED 8th Sept. 1864.

1. We say that, after the filing of our former answer in this cause, that is to say, on the 30th day of May last, the Board of Trustees of the said College duly passed the following resolutions, that is to say, First:—" That the action of the Board as recorded in the minutes of the " 28th January, 1863, generally, and specifying that the action of the Board in the adoption of the " Statutes, Rules and Ordinances for the government of this institution, and the said Statutes, " Rules and Ordinances be now approved and confirmed." Second,—" That the proceedings of " the Board of Trustees at its several meetings on the 9th and 10th days of February last, and " all the particulars thereof be, and are hereby approved and confirmed, more especially as " regards the removal of Professor Weir from his office of Professor of Classics, and Secretary " to the Senatus of the College."

2. The said resolutions were passed after discussion and deliberation by a majority of eleven votes, their having been twenty-one Trustees present besides the chairman.

3. Insisting that the acts of the Board of Trustees questioned in the Bill for irregularity were, and are regular and valid, we submit that such acts are now, beyond all questions, confirmed and made valid and binding on all parties concerned by the resolutions of the Board hereinbefore set forth.

4. We further submit that the Plaintiff has been lawfully and properly dismissed and removed from his said office, and pray to be hence dismissed with all costs of suit.

J. McLENNAN.

4

THE ANSWER OF THE DEFENDANTS, QUEEN'S COLLEGE AT KINGSTON, TO THE AMENDED BILL OF COMPLAINT.

Filed 23rd September, 1864.

In answer to the said amended Bill, we say as follows:—

1. We say that the meeting referred to in our supplemental answer in this cause, and in the twenty-second section of the said amended Bill, was legally and properly convened and held, and that the proper notices required by the charter in that behalf, were given within the time and in manner required thereby.

2. We further rely upon all the defences set up in our former answers in this cause, and on any defences disclosed in the answers of our Co-defendants that may be applicable to our case.

Order *pro confesso* against the Defendants, The Rev. Wm, Inglis and George Malloch, dated 7th May, 1864.

Do. do. against the Defendants, John Thompson and John Greenshields, dated 19th May, 1864.

Do do. against the Defendants, The Reverend John McMornie and Edward Malloch, dated 26th May, 1864.

Replication filed 18th June, 1864.

The Plaintiff in this cause joins issue with all the Defendants herein, except the Defendants The Reverend John McMornie, Edward Malloch, John Thompson, John Greenshields, George Malloch, and The Reverend William Maxwell Inglis, against whom the Plaintiff's Bill has been taken *pro confesso*, and as to such last named Defendants, the Plaintiff will hear this cause on the order *pro confesso*.

Dated this eighteenth day of June, 1864.

CROOKS, KINGSMILL & CATTANACH,

Plaintiff's Solicitors.

Replication filed 19th September, 1864.

The Plaintiff in this cause joins issue with all the Defendants herein, except the Defendants The Reverend John McMornie, Edward Malloch, John Thompson, John Greenshields, George Malloch, and The Reverend William Maxwell Inglis, against whom the Plaintiff's Bill has been taken *pro confesso*, and as to such last named Defendants, the Plaintiff will hear this cause on the order *pro confesso*.

Dated this nineteenth day of September, 1864.

CROOKS, KINGSMILL & CATTANACH,

Plaintiff's Solicitors.

was Rector of the Banff Academy, at Banff, in Scotland. It is called Grammar School and Academy. I was so engaged as Rector for two years and upwards. I was engaged for life *ad vitam ad culpam*. I had a written agreement which so stated it. The extract of it is in the hands of my solicitor, Mr. Crooks, the original is entered in the books of the Banff Academy. I put the extract into the hands of my solicitor before this suit was commenced, as I wanted to shew him that I left a permanent employment in Scotland. The reason why this extract is not mentioned in my affidavit on production of documents is, the I did not see it mentioned in the list my solicitors prepared for me to swear to, and therefore did not mention it, thinking it not to be material, as my solicitor appeared to consider it not to be material. At the time of my making the affidavit I had not that document in my mind. (Mr. McLennan proposes the question " Do you believe that the extract referred to has a bearing on this suit." Mr. Weir answers: " I do not know whether it has or not, I mean to say by this that I cannot express any decided belief at present. The document is an extract of my appointment as Rector of the Banff Academy and Grammar School, at Banff, certified by the Town Clerk, George Forbes, as being a true copy. The extract contains the whole matter of the agreement. My appointment continued on the same terms during the whole time of my being Rector, excepting that the whole departments of the school were put under me instead of the Classical and Mathematical departments alone, when I first entered on my appointment. I was appointed originally as Rector. The words *ad vitam ant culpam* do occur in the extract. There was no other written agreement or instrument that I am aware of. I do not know how the Banff Academy is endowed. I never told any person that my appointment at Banff was not permanent. I never said so to Mrs. Logie, at Kingston. I have no recollection of any conversation with Mrs. Logie, respecting the Banff Academy, at all. It would not make me doubt the accuracy of my recollection, if Mrs. Logie said I had told her so. I got the extract when I entered on my duties at Banff. I have had it in my possession ever since. I do not know who my immediate predecessor was. I have no other document that I am aware of bearing upon the suit, excepting the extract and those produced. It was partly through a communication with Mr. Menzies that I came out here to be Professor. I think there may be one or two letters from Mr. Menzies bearing upon my appointment in Queen's College, which I have lost. I kept no account of them, as I thought them of no importance. I never was at the Edinburgh University as student. My agreement as to my Professorship in Queen's College, was as to my being Professor at a certain salary. The agreement was made with the Trustees, as I suppose. There was no particular agreement that I know of, except that I was to be Professor at a particular salary. In my agreement there was no reference that I know of as to the terms of such Professorship in Edinburgh University. There was no arrangement as to the duration of the agreement. My appointment, so far as I know, was in no wise different to the appointment of the other Professors of Queen's College. I do not know that there was any arrangement that it should be the same as the other Professors. I was simply appointed at a salary of £350 a year.

The grounds of my belief that the major part of the Trustees before the meeting were influenced and prejudiced, as mentioned in the 17th paragraph of the Bill, are as follows :—Dr. Leitch and Mr. Murray, as I had been informed, had, during the Christmas holidays, gone round amongst the Trustees, and had so influenced and prejudiced them. I was informed on the Friday before the ninth of February, that charges were to be brought against me, and that I was to be dismissed without a hearing. I was again informed of the same fact on the Saturday previous to the ninth February, that this was to be done, and that one of the Trustees had seen the charges against me in a lawyer's office in this city. I was further informed that it had been stated by one or two Trustees, previous to the meeting of the ninth, that they were coming

up for the express purpose of dismissing me. I was further informed that the Trustees at a distance had been written to by a Trustee or Trustees in Kingston about this matter; and I was further aware there were some Trustees who knew nothing of the object of the meeting of the ninth. I got the information from several parties. I cannot associate the names of the informants with the particular fact. I speak generally of John May, Charles Peters, William Maxwell Inglis, John Creighton, Judge Malloch, Dr. Cook. On reflection, there may be others whom I do not remember just now. I am not sure that I cannot say for certain that the information as to the meeting of the ninth came through Mr. May. The information that came to me from May came to him from Mrs. Weir. The information that came to me through Peters was, that he had heard that the charges upon which I was to be dismissed, had been seen in a lawyer's office in the city. I am not sure who told Mr. Peters. (Mr. McLennan puts this question " Do you believe you know who gave Mr. Peters the information." The answer given is, " I do not know." (The witness refuses to answer as to his belief.) I got a deal of information from Mr. Inglis. Mr. Inglis told me, to the best of my recollection, in the presence of Mr. Barnett, of Hamilton, that he had been written to by Mr. Morris and Dr. Urquhart, of Cornwall, relative to my dismissal, before the meeting took place, and that this sentence was in the letter, "That the Montreal men had come to an agreement that Weir must be got quit of." I cannot for certain give all the particulars I heard from Judge Malloch. I heard him say that he thought it was a conspiracy to get quit of me. He also said he had no notice of the object of the meeting beyond the general words of the chairman's letter. Dr. Cook stated that while he was here as Principal, means had been taken to prejudice him against me. John Creighton told me, as far as I remember, that on the morning of the ninth, Duncan Morrison, of Brockville, had stated, in the presence of Mr. Inglis, that they had come up with a view of dismissing me. Upon reflection, I do not know of any other persons who gave me information relating to the seventeenth paragraph. I heard rumours about Dr. Leitch's health before the meeting of the ninth February. I heard various rumours about his health. I was aware that, at the meeting of the ninth February, Dr. Leitch was not present. I do not at present remember that any Trustee told me that he had been influenced by Dr. Leitch. I heard of several Trustees being influenced by the document which Dr. Leitch had caused to be read against me. I heard that he had influenced some of the Trustees when on his tour among them during the Christmas holidays. I have not been appointed, that I am aware, to any situation in Quebec. I have not been offered any appointment in Quebec. I am not aware of any change that has taken place in the staff of teachers in Morrin College, Quebec. The Principal of Morrin College has not proposed to me any appointment. (Mr. Weir refuses to answer any questions as to what he had heard respecting changes in Professors or teachers in Morrin College.) I know nothing certain regarding contemplated changes in Morrin College. (Mr. McLennan asks, have you any knowledge of any change, actual or contemplated, in the staff of teachers in Morrin College, Quebec.) Mr. Weir replies, I have no certain knowledge of any change, actual or contemplated, in Morrin College, Quebec. I am not aware who are Governors or Trustees of the College. I had a letter from Dr. Cook respecting an appointment in Morrin College. I am not sure that I have that letter. I do not know whether it is in existence or not; it may possibly be among my papers. I have no reason to suspect it may not be among my papers still. My answer to Dr. Cook was, that I could not entertain the acceptance of any situation in Morrin College, pending the suit with the Trustees. I do not know that soon after I came that Reverend Dr. George was Vice-Principal. I never saw his appointment. I am aware of his having been styled Vice-Principal. He may have been so styled in the minutes of the Senatus Academicus, in my own handwriting. I am not aware that there was any actual Vice-Principal of the College at the time of my appointment. I do not know that Dr. George performed the functions of the Principal. He presided at the meetings

5

of the Senate after I was appointed. Professor Smith was one of my brother Professors. I had no difficulty with Professor Smith while he was Professor, nor any disagreement; we got on harmoniously together. We never had much intercourse. We never came into collision together. I never had any difficulty with him about the examination of the students in my class, or about any books which he brought from Great Britain for me. There was a disagreement between Dr. George and me. It began in the fall of 1856, and was about Mr. Borthwick. Dr. George wished to expel Borthwick from the College. Borthwick was a teacher in the Preparatory School, also a student in Dr. George's class in Theology, for having written a letter in connection with the College. I lodged in the Senatus six reasons against the Senate taking up the question. The complaint of Dr. George was, that Borthwick had published a complaint against the College, calumnious, libellous and false. I took no part further than lodging my six reasons of dissent. I was a matter for the Presbytery, not for them. Dr. George refused to recognise or speak to me after. Dr. George gave no reason to me for so doing. I never heard from Professor George what the reasons were. I surmised it was because I had lodged the six reasons of dissent in the Borthwick matter. No further action was taken in the Borthwick matter by the Senatus. I went to George's house on business. I would have met Dr. George on amicable terms. I was quite willing. Dr. George would not meet me. He gave no reason. The matter came up before the Trustees. Dr. George gave as a reason, that I had taken up a falsehood and supported it. He said I had homologated falsehoods. I claimed protection from the Trustees. He may have had relation to the Borthwick affair, as I suppose. I heard that Dr. George had said that I had a hand in the Borthwick letter. I have so understood that this was the cause of the disagreement between me and George, but it was an insufficient one. He intimated to a committee appointed to deal between me and George, that I was the author of the letter. I was not the author of the letter. I had no part whatever in its preparation. I did not advise its preparation, or any part of it. It was not submitted to me before its publication. I was not privy to its publication. I am not aware that I discussed with Mr. Borthwick, the propriety of such a publication. I did not discuss the propriety of such a publication with Mr. Borthwick. I had not any knowledge that such a publication was contemplated. I had no reason to suspect such a publication. The interruption of friendly relations continued up to the 12th November, 1859, or thereabouts. The letter may, to some extent, have caused some excitement and discussion amongst the Professors and students of the College. I am not aware that it continued during the time of the disagreement between Dr. George and me. I brought the matter prominently before the students. I was informed there had been a meeting of the students, at which a violent speech had been made against me by a student, the now Rev. Robert Campbell, of Galt, then head master of the Preparatory School. I then brought the matter before the students. I did call a meeting of the students for the purpose of vindicating my own character, which had been assailed, as I heard, at a previous meeting of the students. The first meeting was called for the purpose of considering the propriety of presenting me with a testimonial as Professor. After class hours I intimated to the members of my class that I would meet them to explain the matters in which my character had been so gravely assailed at the previous meeting of students. I stated that all the students of the College might attend who chose. I gave no further notice to the students who did not belong to my class. The meeting was held, and I addressed the students, and laid the whole of the Borthwick case before the students. I did not address the students on the subject of the difficulties between me and Dr. George. I made the misrepresentation of me by Robert Campbell also a subject of my remarks. I did not refer in any manner to the conduct of the Trustees. I may have spoken in private with students respecting the Borthwick matter. I believe there was a difference in my class among the students as to the differences between me and Dr. George. I do not know there were two parties in my class.

For aught I know, there was no division of opinion in my class. The Borthwick matter was up as I have heard, on several occasions before the Trustees. I was present on the Trustee Board when the matter was finally settled. After this Borthwick matter there was a correspondence between me and George. Professor George and I became reconciled on the 12th November, 1859. We met after that, as far as I am concerned, in a friendly manner. I could not tell what Dr. George's feelings were to me from that time forth. In 1861, another difficulty occurred between us. The cause was, that Dr. George had seduced my sister, as I had been informed. I wrote him that when in Scotland, in 1861, I heard that in 1874 he had seduced my sister. I did this at the instance of my brother, without my sister's knowledge. I did not address the students of the College on this matter. I was not present at any meeting of students when the matter of this difficulty with Professor George was discussed. There were three or four students at my house when they asked me questions about the matter, and I answered them. I have no remembrance of speaking to the students, unless they put the questions first to me. When questions were put to me respecting the charge against Dr. George, I gave an explanation, and vindicated myself respecting the course I had taken. I was asked by these students if it was true that I had brought a false charge against Dr. George. I told them the evidence would shew that it was not a false charge. I did say to the students when they asked me, that I would lay the whole matter before them. I shewed them the evidence, that is the affidavits of my sister, of Mrs. Leckie, and of Mrs. Patrick Weir. I have no remembrance of anything more. I showed them the correspondence between me and Dr. George. I have no remembrance of showing any letter from my sister. This occurred once. I think three students were present. I am not sure as to their names. To the best of my recollection the students were Alexander McQuatrie, John McMillan. I do not remember the third just now. I have no recollection of any other conversation on the matter with several students. I may have conversed with other students at my own house, when questioned by them. I have no recollection of exhibiting the documents to my students, but on the above-mentioned occasion. I never conversed in any of the College class-rooms with any of the students on this matter. I never addressed the students in the College class-room on the matter. In the year 1862, at the close of session, one of the students asked me if I was to be examiner in classics. My answer was, I did not know, that I had been placed in a painful position, and I said some of the Trustees were of the same opinion. I read extract of letters from Dr. Cook and Mr. Burnet, to the effect that I should never have been placed in the painful position in which I was. I brought the charge against Dr. George before the Trustees. They took no action whatever, Dr. George having previously resigned. He resigned in December, 1861. I am not aware of having discussed the action of the Trustees before the students. I am not aware of having spoken to the students about the action of the Trustees. I never spoke to the students of my class about the action of the Trustees. I am not aware of exhibiting these papers to any private person not connected with the College, except my lawyer. I have no remembrance of reading the papers to any private person not connected with the College. I never advised any student not to attend Dr. George's class. I never refused or omitted to attend meetings of senatus because Dr. George would be present. I cannot say whether I did or did not relate this charge to my acquaintances—private persons. It did not often happen that I discussed this matter with private individuals. I have answered questions about it when put to me. I have not been in the habit of relating the particulars of these matters to private indi-viduals. I was on friendly terms with the late Principal Dr. Leitch. I know nothing to the contrary. We met in a friendly way, on speaking terms. On my part there was no unfriendly relation. I cannot say for his part. Dr. Leitch found fault with my conduct in reference to a meeting of the senatus. He blamed me for calling the meeting wrongly. I am not aware that I have spoken disrespectfully of Dr. Leitch. I am not aware that I applied to him the epithet

dut
to
au
I w
inti
not
Let
be
res
sen
pre
Wil
tha
dise
olo
nev
wri
kine
aho
Ecl
pri
one
wro
the
dist
idea
Wh
kno
Esh
was
kno
to p
I to
ach
the
man
sen
is no
if th
the
Pato
in w
Trus

of " Janus." I am not aware that I ever ridicul of the Principal. I believe I never did. I am not aware that I ever spoke to the students, or any particular student, blamingly of Dr. Leitch's conduct. I never, during 1861 or 1862, absented myself from my class, unless from illness. I never discharged my office of superintendent of schools to the neglect of my class. I never neglected my classes. I was never absent from my classes for the purpose of attending to my duties as School Superintendent. I was one week absent, very sick. I was unfit, from illness, to teach, and on one afternoon of that week I visited a school or schools as Superintendent. I am not sure I was a week absent. I cannot say whether I went to one or more of the schools. I was not required by the Trustees to give up my post as Superintendent of schools. It was intimated to me that the Trustees thought it did interfere with my duties as Professor. I did not give up being Superintendent. I am Superintendent still. I do not remember that Dr. Leitch offered to take my place in teaching my class when I was ill. He said my place could be supplied. I gave him no answer further than that I expected soon to be back myself. I have no recollection of saying anything disrespectful on my part to the Principal during the meeting of senatus. At a meeting, Dr. Williamson, a Professor, had some discussion in the Principal's presence respecting the impropriety of writing notes on backs of old used envelopes. Professor Williamson said it was not a proper way of dealing with the Professors of the College. I said that he, the Principal, had done the same to me; that I did not set it down to any personal discourtesy to me, but that I set it down to his not knowing better. I did not make slighting observations of that kind to the Principal. I do not consider that a slighting observation. I never wrote anonymous contributions about the College on any subject, or procured them to be written or printed, or was privy to such. I never charged the Principal with misconduct of any kind. I am not aware that I did. I never proposed to other persons to write communications about the College, so that I might answer them. I know the contents of the paper marked Exhibit No. 1. The extract on the first page was sent to me by the Trustees. I have seen the printed matter on the second page. I saw it at a meeting of the Trustees, produced by Mr. Paton, one of the Trustees. It was in part got up by me. I do not remember when it was got up. I wrote some of the paragraphs on the second page. I rather think I did not write the whole of the paragraph. I do not know who prepared the remainder. I am not sure. I have no very distinct belief about it. I am not sure who had any business about it besides me. I have no idea how many persons were concerned besides me in getting it up. I got the whole printed. When printed, I did nothing with them. When printed, they were sent to my house. I do not know what was done with them after they came to my house. I did not write the address on Exhibit No. 1. I have no recollection how many were printed. I got this ready to show what was the real decision of the Trustees in Dr. George's case. I paid for the printing. I do not know how many were printed. I cannot say if there were a hundred. I swear I took no steps to put them in circulation. I surmise they might have been taken from my house and circulated. I took the manuscript to the printer. I am not sure from whom I received the manuscript of such parts as I did not write. I swear upon my oath that I am not sure from whom I received the manuscript. I swear upon my oath that I do not know who composed the remainder of the manuscript, or any part of the remainder. I did not suggest as to whom the notices were to be sent. I do not suppose that the original manuscript of the printed matter on the second page is not in existence. I have no reason to suppose one way or the other about it. I do not know if the printer's manuscript was all in my own handwriting. I do not know in whose handwriting the manuscript of the matter in the second page is. It is not in my handwriting. I heard Mr. Paton say that the notice sent to Dr. George was in my handwriting. I never heard other in whose handwriting it was. I never, in my class, read any papers bearing upon the acts of the Trustees. I have no idea in whose handwriting the Exhibit No. 1 is addressed. I do not know

the handwriting. I have seen the document marked (*Exhibit No. 2.*) I was not in the least matter concerned with the publication of this document. I do not know when I first saw it. It first came under my notice when I saw it in my own house. I cannot say when that was. I cannot tell how it came to my house. I cannot say that I saw it with anybody, but I saw it for the first time in my own house. Nobody told me how it came there. I am not aware that I asked anybody where it came from. I read it when first I saw it. I cannot say in what part of my house I first saw it. I may have seen it in manuscript. I think I did see it in manuscript. I may have seen it before publication. I cannot say if I read it in manuscript or not. I may have done so. After I read it I did not put it anywhere. I have read it in my own house; it may have been read to me, I am not certain. I cannot say how many copies of Exhibit No. 2 I have seen. I never counted how many I have seen in my house. I may possibly have seen a dozen. I do not know that I have seen fifty. I could not swear I had not. I would not swear I had seen a hundred copies in my own house. I will not swear that I have not seen as many as two hundred. I will not swear as to any number. I rather think I do not now know the handwriting of the manuscript. I will not swear that I did not know the handwriting of the manuscript when I first saw it. I am not perfectly sure who composed it. I am not perfectly sure that I know who composed any part of it. I do not know who paid for the printing of it. I do not know any person who contributed any funds towards the expense of printing. I do not know who was the printer. I cannot say how many copies of Exhibit No. 2 I have seen in my house. I cannot tell how they came to my house, or how they came to my house from the printer's office. I do not know if they came from the printer's office to my house. I do not suppose I ever saw a very large number of them together at my house. I have no idea what number I may have seen together at my house. Before this production was published, I was not aware it was to be published. I have not seen any lately at my house. I never saw the proof. I did not furnish any of the materials for it. I may have got a copy through the post-office. I have no recollection of receiving it through the post-office. I was not surprised at seeing the Exhibit No. 2 in my house. I am not aware that I ever asked any body how they came there, or how they went. Nobody ever told me. I do not know if this was in 1862. I have no recollection of causing them to be removed from my house in any manner.

In explanation by Mr. O'REILLY, *for Plaintiff.*

It was also through a communication from Dr. Cook, a Trustee of Queen's College, who visited Scotland, that I came out here to be a Professor. I remember now who my immediate predecessor at the Banff Academy was. His name was, I think, Leask. (Mr. Weir desires to explain that the statement is made by me. "There was no particular agreement made with the Trustees that I know of" this wise.) That in 1852, Dr. Cook, one of the Trustees of Queen's College, when speaking of my coming to Canada as a Professor, gave me distinctly to understand that the tenure of the Professorships in Queen's College were similar to that in the Scottish Universities, (to which Defendants' counsel objected as not being in explanation, and which explanation was overruled.) I explain, Mr. Menzies also, in one or other of his letters, gave me the same assurance that the tenure of the Professorships in Queen's College was similar to that in the Scottish Universities. I explain that Dr. Cook told me that while he was here as Principal, means had been taken to prejudice him against me on the part of the then Secretary to the Board of Trustees, and one or more of the Trustees, resident in Kingston. I also explain that I submitted to the students my connection with the Borthwick case, in which I had been misrepresented to them instead of "that I laid the whole of the Borthwick case before the students."

6

I

G.

Fe
in
Fe
So
pro
wri
Do
ing
tice
him
him
be t
had
lega
conv
The
amou
being
tinue
of th

I would also explain, that I did not address the students on the subject of the difficulties between me and Dr. George, except so far only as related to the Borthwick case. I further explain, that Dr. George laid the matter of my charge of seducing my sister before the Trustees, demanding an investigation, and accusing me of bringing a false charge against him, and that was the cause of the publicity given to it by me to the students. (Overruled as not being in explanation, Mr. McLennan also objects.) I also explain, that I showed the correspondence between me and Dr. George, after Dr. George resigned, and caused the correspondence to be laid before the Trustees, and not till then. I also explain, that I was not required by the Trustees to give up my post of Superintendent of Schools, as I understood the document sent to me by the Trustees. I also explain, that I never wrote anonymous contributions about the College, on any subject, or procured them to be written or printed, or was privy to such, except as to a paper similar to Exhibit No. 1.

(Signed,)   GEORGE WEIR.

DEPOSITIONS OF WITNESSES TAKEN AT KINGSTON, 26th, 27th and 28th SEPT., 1864.

PLAINTIFF'S WITNESSES.

Monday, 26th September, 1864.

GEORGE MALLOCH, a Defendant, sworn:

I am one of the Trustees of Queen's College, I believe, and was so, I believe, in the month of February last. I have been a Trustee for a number of years. I have attended frequently the meetings of the Trustees. I was present at the meeting of the Trustees of the ninth and tenth of February, 1864. A paper in reference to the Plaintiff was read at this meeting by Judge Logie. Some action on it was proposed in regard to Plaintiff. I opposed this, as the Plaintiff was not present, and I considered that the meeting was illegally convened, as I had represented in writing to the Board a week preceding. My objection was over-ruled ; and the action of the Board was had in the absence of Plaintiff, who was not present at the discussion ; nor at the meeting before the vote to remove him was come to. This vote was taken without his having had notice or summons to be present at the meeting. I objected that it was unjust to proceed against him without notice. That the complaint against him ought to have been in writing, and served on him. I objected to the reading by Judge Logie of the paper referred to, as it was said it was to be taken away, and not left among the Records of the College. The Chairman, after the meeting had been opened with prayer, read letters of protest from myself and Dr. Cook against the legality of the meeting. He then read a letter from Dr. Leitch, the Principal, asking him to convene the meeting. Judge Logie then rose to read a written statement affecting the Plaintiff. The Chairman took the sense of the meeting as to whether this written statement was to remain among the College's papers, and it was decided in the negative. And I then objected to its being read. It was matter of complaint at the meeting against the Plaintiff that he had continued to hold the position of Local Superintendent of Schools, contrary to the recommendation of the Board of Trustees. This complaint was withdrawn, as the resolution of the Board in regard

to the subject was not mandatory. Hugh Allan, a Defendant, moved the resolution to dismiss Plaintiff. The resolution was discussed before it was passed. It was passed on the morning of the tenth of February. I was not made aware, previously to its assembly, of the object of the meeting. It was assumed to be an adjourned meeting. I considered it as illegally assembled, as it assumed to be a meeting adjourned from a previous meeting, founded on an assumed adjournment in the previous October, whereas no such adjournment, as I considered, had taken place; and the meeting of February should therefore have been convened on fresh notice, according to the terms of the Charter. I had no notice previously to the meeting of the ninth of February, 1864, that the object of the meeting was to dismiss the Plaintiff. I produce the notice which I received to attend that meeting, (*Exhibit* "*A*.") I produce my answer to that notice, ("*Exhibit h*.")

Cross-examined.—I am aware of a difficulty between the Plaintiff and other authorities of the College, prior to the complaints on which he was removed. Complaints against the Plaintiff, previous to those latter, were made the subject of discussion at a former meeting of the Board. They were verbal charges by Mr. Paton, which it was understood were to be put in writing, and submitted, but were not to be signed. I did not know, previously to the meeting of the ninth of February, 1864, that Professor Weir's conduct or position was to form the subject of discussion. Except on the occasion of the meeting of October, 1863, it had been the practice to adjourn a concluded meeting to some subsequent day. No such adjournment took place of this meeting in October while I was present, though the Minutes of the Board record an adjournment. none such took place before the meeting broke up. Plaintiff had made a complaint against a brother Professor, Mr. George, at a previous meeting. I was in the chair, and refused to receive it, as I considered it irregular. I understood that there were two parties in the College caused by the dissensions between Plaintiff and Professor George. The latter resigned his place in the College. I have heard members of the Board individually say that it would be better to get rid of Professor Weir, the Plaintiff, in consequence of the difficulties in the College, of which, however, I did not think the Plaintiff was the cause. Professor George had resigned some time before Plaintiff was removed.

(Signed,)   GEO. MALLOCH.

WILLIAM IRELAND, sworn :

I am Secretary to the Board of Trustees of Queen's College in Kingston, Defendants in this suit, and I produce a book containing Minutes of Proceedings of the board of the ninth and tenth of February, 1864. It is Minute Book Number Two. I was present at those proceedings and recorded the Minutes of them. They are correct. The meeting of the ninth of February was assumed to be a meeting adjourned from the previous third of February, when there was a meeting of three of the Trustees only, and this meeting was adjourned from a meeting held on the sixth of January previously, which had been adjourned from the previous sixth of December, the meeting on which day was by adjournment from the fourth of November previously, which meeting was held, as assumed, by adjournment from a meeting of the second of October previously. The meeting of the second of October was adjourned *sine die*. The meeting of the first of October was held pursuant to an adjournment of the ordinary General Meeting held on the sixteenth of September previously. The meeting of the second of October, which commenced its sittings on the first of October, was a Special Meeting. On the first of October the ordinary General Meeting was also held, and was adjourned till the fourth of November. I produce the Minutes of the meeting of the seventh May, 1862. On the eighth of May, 1862, the Board disposed of certain charges made against the Plaintiff by Mr. Paton. On the twelfth day of December,

1861, the resignation of his place in the College by Professor George was accepted and recorded among the minutes of the Board. On the thirty-first of May, 1864, a meeting of the Board was held. Its proceedings were recorded in the Minute Book Number Two. The meeting was convened by circulars signed by the Chairman, a copy of which I produce. (*Exhibit " C."*) They were addressed to the members of the Board, and mailed by myself on the twenty-ninth of April, 1864. I did not, but the Chairman did, advertise in The Kingston News, a notice of this meeting. I was not directed to insert any such advertisement. I look at a letter signed by Mr. Paton, addressed to the Plaintiff, dated the twelfth of November, 1859. (*Exhibit " D."*) I produce a minute of the Proceedings of the Board on the tenth of November, 1859. I produce a minute of Proceedings of the Board on the twentieth of July, 1853. (*Minute Book No. 2.*) The resolutions then adopted authorize the employment of Plaintiff as Classical Professor. The usual way of employing Professors and Officers is by resolution of the Trustees. On the twenty-first of January, 1863, the draft of certain statutes affecting the College was presented. On the twenty-sixth of January, 1863, they were discussed and adopted by the Board. On the second of October, 1863, a motion was made to rescind some of these statutes. They were referred to the consideration of a Committee, which has not yet reported. The Minutes of the Board (Minute Book Number Two) shew all this. On the ninth of March, 1864, Mr. Paton and Mr. Inglis were appointed a Committee to prepare the Annual Report to the Colonial Committee of the General Assembly of the Church of Scotland. They made a Report, and despatched it, as appears from the Minute of the twenty-eighth of April, 1864. I produce a printed copy of the Statutes adopted by the Board in regard to the College. I was present at the meetings of the ninth and tenth of February last in my capacity as Secretary. The Trustees, whose names appear in the Minutes of that date, were present. There was not much discussion about Plaintiff; very few spoke. Mr. Paton stated that, in his judgment, the College would not be worked harmoniously so long as Plaintiff was retained in it. I do not think that the character of the discussion influenced the action of those present. I saw in possession of Judge Logie the written statement referred to by last witness. I never saw it out of his possession. It was said to have emanated from Dr. Leitch, the Principal of the College. It was made a matter of complaint against Plaintiff that he had continued to act as Local Superintendent of Schools contrary to the orders of the Board. On inquiry it was found that there was no such order, but merely a recommendation. I heard no other complaint than this, and what Mr. Paton stated against Plaintiff. If there was any other it must have been stated very shortly, and did not attract my attention. On the morning of the tenth the resolution of the Board to remove Plaintiff was come to without any discussion on that day. A legal opinion was first read in regard to the tenure of office by Plaintiff. I had no information in regard to the object of this meeting than what is contained in the circular notices to the members. I was handed the manuscript notice by Mr. Paton, with instructions to have it printed and circulated. I produce this—(*Exhibit " F"*)—it is in the handwriting of Mr. Alexander Morris, a Defendant. I produce a printed circular of the fifth of February, 1861, for the meeting of the ninth of February. By a Minute of the ninth of November, 1859, Dr. Leitch was appointed Principal of the College. A Minute of the eighth and ninth of August, 1861, has reference to a letter from Dr. Leitch on the subject of his office. I produce that letter, dated the tenth of July, 1861, addressed to (*Exhibit " H."*) This letter was referred to the consideration of a Committee. I have been Secretary of the Board continuously from June, 1861. I had been Secretary at a former period. Judge Malloch objected that the meeting of the eighth and ninth and tenth of February was illegal. Two letters on the subject of the nature of the tenure of Dr. Leitch's office in the College were read to the Board, one from Mr. Morris (*Exhibit " J."*) dated 3rd August, 1861, the other from Mr. Logie (a Defendant), dated the sixth August, 1861. (*Exhibit " K."*) Mr. Paton (a Defendant) is

Treasurer of the College. The College Fund was founded by donations which have been invested. It receives an Annual Grant from the Colonial Committee of the Church of Scotland, and also from the Provincial Legislature. The Professor of Classical Literature receives a salary of One Thousand Five Hundred Dollars per annum. Since Plaintiff's removal an Interim Lecturer has been appointed, as appears by a Minute of the third of August, 1864. I believe the Professorship of Classical Literature has existed since the opening of the College.

Cross-examined.—The Minutes of the first of October, 1853, record the receipt of letters from two of the Trustees announcing Mr. Weir's acceptance of the Professorship of Classical Literature in the College. The Minute of the eighth of June, 1854, records the confirmation of the appointment of Plaintiff to such office. I am not aware of any instrument of appointment, or of any other act than the resolutions of the Board referred to nominating the Plaintiff. No Professor has been appointed otherwise than by resolution, that I am aware of. In the discussions on the ninth of February, 1864, there was no temper or ill feeling displayed towards Mr. Weir, further than may be implied in the remark attributed to Mr. Paton. There was no specific charge made against Plaintiff, other than I have mentioned. I remember Mr. Neilson, of Belleville, stating that a gentleman in his neighbourhood had stated that he would not send his son to the College so long as Mr. Weir was in it. This meeting of the ninth of February commenced its sittings at seven in the evening, and continued till twelve o'clock at night, and was then adjourned till next morning. The time of the meeting was principally occupied with the case of the Plaintiff, though there were other matters discussed. Mr. Weir complained that the Trustees had not investigated the charges against Professor George. From time to time, at meetings of the Board, individual members complained of the conduct of Plaintiff in the College. The meeting of the ninth and tenth of February, was held by regular adjournments of previous meetings. It has always been the practice to adjourn the usual regular meetings, and notice is given to all the members of the time of such adjourned meetings, if the subject be of importance. If there be not a quorum of five at any meeting, an adjournment to a subsequent day takes place. The meeting of the thirty-first of May, 1864, as per Minute of that date, confirms the Minutes of the ninth and tenth of February, and the dismissal of Plaintiff. This meeting of the thirty-first of May, was upon the requisition of three Trustees, and was advertised in the *Kingston News*, and circular notices of it sent to members. It was also an adjourned meeting. The resolution of the thirty-first of May was carried by fifteen votes to four. The resolution of the tenth of February, 1864, was carried by thirteen votes to two. All the meetings of the Board relating to Plaintiff's appointment and dismissal, were adjourned meetings of the Board. The meeting of the twentieth of July, 1853, was a regularly adjourned meeting following from an adjourned meeting on the fifteenth of October, 1851, at which there was no quorum. The meeting of the eighth June, 1854, at which Plaintiff's appointment was confirmed, also followed from the adjourned meeting of the fifteenth of October, 1851. It has not been usual to obtain the requisition of three Trustees for calling a meeting of the Board. There were two meetings on the first of October, 1861; the one a meeting specially called, the other the usual ordinary meeting, which was adjourned over as already stated during the recess of the special meeting. There was no quorum present at the adjournment. The chairman alone was present. Mr. Weir was not present at the meeting of the thirty-first of May, 1864, nor had he any notice to be present. There was a great deal of discussion at this meeting in regard to Plaintiff. He knew nothing of it that I am aware of. No specific charges were made against him at this meeting. I hand in a letter from Dr. Cook, (*Exhibit* " L,") with enclosures 1 and 2. I hand in a letter of Dr. Cook, (*Exhibit* " M",) and a letter of Hugh Allan, (*Exhibit* " N".) I also produce a letter from Dr. Cook, (*Exhibit* " O.")

(Signed,)   W. IRELAND.

Tuesday, 27th September, 1864.

CHARLES PETERS, sworn :

I am a School-Teacher in Kingston, and received my education in King's College, Aberdeen, and at the University of Edinburgh. It is considered that the appointment of a Professor in the Scottish Universities is a permanent one—for life. I knew Plaintiff in Scotland first at King's College, Aberdeen. Plaintiff was a prominent student there. My first personal acquaintance with him was in Banff, when he was Rector of the Banff Academy. At this Institution, Students were prepared for College. There were four Masters in the Academy.—Plaintiff was at the head of it. Plaintiff was first appointed to the Classical and Mathematical chairs, and after six months he was put at the head of the Academy. George Forbes was Town Clerk of Banff in 1850. I look at a paper signed by him. (*Exhibit "P."*) I saw it in Banff, in possession of Plaintiff, and I have since seen it here. Plaintiff continued in the Academy in Banff about two years and a half, when, having been offered the Professorship of Classics in Queen's College here, he left it. His reputation in Banff, as a Teacher and Master, was very high indeed.

(Signed.)   C. PETERS.

ALEXANDER LOGIE, sworn :

I am one of the Defendants. I remember the meeting of the Trustees of the ninth and tenth of February last. I produced and read at that meeting, a written statement referred to by the other witnesses. I received it from Dr. Leitch. It was, I believe, in his handwriting. I gave it, after reading it, to Mr. Morris, or Mr. Paton to return to Dr. Leitch. I had promised the latter to return it to him after reading it. I have no reason to doubt that he received it back.— He never afterwards called upon me for it.

(Signed)   A. LOGIE.

JOHN PATON, sworn as a Defendant :

I was present at the meeting of the Trustees of the ninth and tenth of February last. I saw the statement in writing referred to by the last witness, and read by him at the meeting, in the possession of Dr. Leitch after the meeting.

(Signed,)   JOHN PATON.

JOHN COOK, sworn as a Defendant :

I am a Doctor of Divinity, and a Graduate of the University of Glasgow, and have been an ordained Minister of the Church of Scotland for twenty-eight years. I took a prominent part in the establishment of Queen's College, and am one of the Trustees named in the Royal Charter which I proceeded to England to obtain, and did obtain. The endowment of the College consisted of gifts and subscriptions, the largest of which were obtained in Quebec. They were provided almost exclusively by members of the Church of Scotland. Annual collections are made for bursaries in the College. A chair of Classical Literature was one of the first established in the College. Mr. Campbell, at present of the University of Aberdeen, was the first Classical Master. He resigned his office here for a place in the Church in Scotland. The vacancy

of t
to f
of
thei
Prof
for
I wa
I wa
his
fess
sequ
Gran
ted.
rem
been
land,
state
sequ

occurred in 1852. I was requested by the Trustees to make enquiries for a successor to him. I consulted Professor Menzies, of the University of Edinburgh, who had an intimate knowledge of the capacities of the different teachers of three counties, and no one could be better qualified to form a judgment. He recommended two teachers, Professor Geddes, now of the University of Aberdeen, and the Plaintiff. I had communicated with these two gentlemen, and thought very highly of both. My own view then was, and always has been, that a Professorship in Queen's College, was a life appointment. Mr. Weir, the Plaintiff, was selected for the appointment. I look at a letter in the handwriting of Mr. Menzies, (*Exhibit "O."*) I was Principal of Queen's College during the session of 1857 to 1858, and part of 1858 to 1859. I was thus brought into close contact with the Plaintiff. I considered that he was discharging his duties efficiently. I had no difficulty with him. A difficulty arose between Plaintiff and Professor George, in, or previously to 1859. Dr. George had been acting as Principal, and in consequence of this difficulty it was that I became Principal in 1859. Dr. George was a man of firmness, and inclined to have his own way. The difficulty between him and Plaintiff was adjusted. Excepting this difficulty, everything worked harmoniously in the College. Dr. George resumed his duties of " fessor of Divinity after the difficulty between him and Plaintiff had been settled, and ev , aing, so far as I know, went on well till after Plaintiff's return from Scotland, when Dr. George, in a letter to the Board, complained that Plaintiff was circulating statements injurious to his character, and demanding an investigation. This was not had in consequence of Dr. George resigning his position in the College at the end of the session. Subsequently a series of charges growing out of the difficulties between Plaintiff and Dr. George, was preferred against the Plaintiff to the Board, by Mr. Paton. These charges were disposed of by the Board at a meeting on the eighth of May, 1862. I was present thereat. There was much discussion. Dr. Leitch succeeded me as Principal. I was not present at the meeting of the ninth and tenth of February, 1864. I had protested against the legality of the meeting, as I did not think it was called according to the terms of the Charter. I also objected to its being assembled on a Tuesday, when Wednesday had been the usual day of meeting. I heard by telegram, from Professor Weir, on the Saturday previously, that he was to be brought before the Board. I was present at the meeting of the thirty-first of May, 1864. I strongly objected to the action of the Board in regard to the Plaintiff. My objections were not answered. There was no discussion, I think, by those opposed to the Plaintiff. I think that very strong feelings were aroused by the dispute between Professor George and the Plaintiff. I think it was impossible for a Trustee living in Kingston, not to side with the one or the other. Mr. Morris, of Montreal, entertained views unfavourable to Dr. George. Mr. Paton took the contrary view. The Professors of the University were considered as doing the work of the Church, by reason of their educating young men in divinity, and were allowed to commute as life members, or as having a life interest in the Clergy Reserve fund by reason of their position in the University. The money in respect of these commuted claims, was paid over to the Church of Scotland, in Canada, and the Church being under pledge to the individuals making these claims, and to the College, held the commuted funds in trust for them and the College. One of the Professors, who thus commuted, having since died, the sum for which he commuted is now held for the benefit of the College. The Plaintiff was one of those who thus commuted. Dr. George has, since his resignation, been held entitled during his life to the benefit of his commutation. The annual sum claimed from this commutation fund, used to make up the salaries of the Professors. They were allowed to commute as ministers doing the work of the Church, and as receiving part of their salaries from the Church. The amount of Plaintiff's commutation was large, between Two Thousand and Three Thousand Pounds, as he was a young man. I think, that subsequent to the resignation of Dr. George, and till the Statutes affecting the tenure of office of Professors were passed, things

were
The
Fund.
life of
opinic
Profec
fessor
by the

of Cla
printo
it befo
of Que
standi
upon
was co
do wi
against
speak
latter
difficul
finally
In 18(
sednce
in Scot
got th
write to
George
he woul
Dr. Ge
Board
for it.'
of the 8
remain
proceed
the chu
position
a prinio
advised
the rem
the meet
a pampl
let was a
at that
getting
to matter
by me.

were working harmoniously in the College. The Statutes gave great offence to the Professors. The consent of the Church was necessary to the individual commutations on the Clergy Reserve Fund. It was part of the arrangement that the individual Professors should have the benefit for life of their commutations, which afterwards were to go to the College. I have not changed my opinion of Plaintiff as a fit and capable person for Professor. I have recommended him for a Professorship in the College in Quebec, of which I am Principal. The tenure of office of Professors in all the Scotch Universities, is "*ad vitam aut culpam*," except so far as it is now affected by the Imperial Act of 1858.

Cross-examined.—In August, 1852, I went to Scotland, and there inquired about a Professor of Classics. The only authority I had was the Minute of the Board in regard to it. I look at a printed pamphlet purporting to contain the Statutes of McGill College, Montreal. I have seen it before. I have no doubt it contains a true copy of those Statutes, (*Exhibit Q.*) The Principal of Queen's College was appointed by the resolution of the Board. There was no express understanding or provision as to their term of office, except in the case of Dr. Leitch, who insisted upon an express agreement as to his term of office, which was given him without difficulty, as it was considered a life appointment. Dr. George charged that Professor Weir had something to do with an anonymous letter addressed to the members of the Church, making complaint against him, Dr. George. He had no proof of this, but he refused to know the Plaintiff, or to speak to him. Plaintiff always professed his readiness to give his hand to Dr. George, but the latter refused, and resigned his place as Professor of Divinity. This was the cause of the first difficulty between Plaintiff and Dr. George, and took place, I think, as early as 1857. It was finally reconciled at a meeting of the Board in 1859. It led to dissensions in and out of College. In 1861, after Professor Weir returned from Scotland, he accused Professor George of having seduced his sister, and had by her a male child, and that he had been so informed by his brother in Scotland, and by his sister. Plaintiff first spoke to me in the matter, and I expressed my regret that he had done so, and advised him to avoid any open difficulty with Dr. George, and to write to him to say that he could not meet him again. This he did, I believe, and Professor George wrote to know what those charges were. He requested Plaintiff to state his charges, and he would defend himself against them, though he intended resigning at the end of the Session. Dr. George demanded that the Board should investigate the matter. This led to publicity. The Board declined unless a written statement of complaint was made by some person responsible for it. A Committee waited upon Dr. George, who stated his intention of resigning at the end of the Session. The Board requested this in writing, which he gave, and then allowed him to remain till the end of the Session, when he resigned, and the Board then held it unnecessary to proceed with the investigation. It was after Dr. George had been called upon officially to meet the charges or resign, that he demanded investigation. Plaintiff declined to put himself in the position of a prosecutor of the charges against Dr. George. This he did by letter. I received a printed paper similar to that now produced, (*Exhibit "R."*) I don't know who sent it to me. I advised the Plaintiff not to write or speak on the subject. I believe Plaintiff was the writer of the remarks on Exhibit " R." (*Exhibit " S."*) The first of the charges preferred by Mr. Paton at the meeting on the eighth of May, 1862, refers to the paper containing these remarks. I received a pamphlet similar to the one now produced, (*Exhibit " T."*) A charge in relation to this pamphlet was also preferred by Mr. Paton at the meeting of the eighth of May, 1862. Plaintiff appeared at that meeting to answer the charges made by Mr. Paton. There was some difficulty about getting witnesses who could not be found. Mr. Creighton refused to answer certain questions as to matters he considered confidential. The resolution of the eighth of May, 1862, was prepared by me. The Plaintiff's commutation was had with him as a Clergyman of the Church, not as a

it wh
seem
of Di
to re
befor

" l "
the cl
and L
an in
then
secut
mem
the C

Jons

I
death.
refere
It is i
ing of
1861,
condu
of Phi
with I.
tion,
Dr. Le
The vi
discus
condu
heard
to the
in Nov
ing pe
the Se
Profess
They
passed
aware,
and Di
to these
I receiv

Professor. It would follow him as a Clergyman while he lived in Canada. The fund is held by the Church, but for the benefit of the College, after the life interests in it are extinct. It is managed by the Body having charge of the Church temporalities. My knowledge of the tenure of office of Professors in the Scotch Universities, is derived from the general opinion in regard to it which prevails in Scotland, and from conversing with those acquainted with the subject. There seems but one opinion about it. I never knew of any other. Unless in the case of a Professor of Divinity, who may be had before the Ecclesiastical Court, it seemed to be almost impossible to remove a Professor in Scotland for any cause. I do not know how it could have been done before the recent Statute.

Re-examined.—I looked at a letter of Plaintiff of the seventh of November, 1863. *Exhibit* " 15." I was misunderstood as to the time at which Dr. George demanded an investigation of the charges made against him by Plaintiff, in 1861. It was after receiving the Plaintiff's letters, and before he had been addressed on the subject, at the instance of the Board, that he demanded an investigation. Dr. George first brought the subject before the Board, and the Plaintiff was then called upon to bring forward his case against Dr. George. Plaintiff having declined to prosecute, and Dr. George having expressed an intention to resign, it was thought by some of the members that the matter would be got rid of by his resignation, and they appointed the Committee to wait upon him.

(Signed,)　　　　JOHN COOK.

JOHN CLARK MURRAY, sworn.

I am the Executor in Canada of the late Dr. Leitch, and took charge of his papers on his death. I have made no investigation of them, but among them I have found a statement in reference to the Plaintiff, and his difficulties with Queen's College. I produce it, (*Exhibit* " 17.") It is in the handwriting of Dr. Leitch, with the exception of a portion, which is in the handwriting of Mr. Machar. I had heard of the intention to call the meeting of the ninth of February, 1861, almost a week before that day. I think I heard it from Dr. Leitch, and that Plaintiff's conduct was to be brought before it. I have been in the company of Trustees when the conduct of Plaintiff formed the subject of conversation, more than a year ago. I was present in company with Drs. Urquhart, Leitch, and Mr. McLean, when it was spoken of during last Christmas vacation. I remember the Plaintiff's conduct forming frequently the subject of conversation between Dr. Leitch and Mr. Paton, and this prior to February last, and for a few months previously. The views of Dr. Leitch were entertained by Mr. Morris, a Defendant, and myself, and were discussed between us. Prior to February, 1864, I had heard great dissatisfaction with Plaintiff's conduct expressed by Drs. Leitch and Urquhart, and Messrs. Paton, Morris and McLean. I heard a wish expressed by these gentlemen that something should be done by the Board in regard to the Plaintiff's conduct. I arrived here to assume my duties as Professor in Queen's College in November, 1862, having received my appointment as such five or six weeks previously. Nothing passed as to the tenure of my office, nor did I ever consider the matter. I am Secretary of the Senate. There was no conference with the Senate, nor with the Professors, since I became Professor here, before the passing of the Statutes affecting the tenure of office by the Professors. They were passed before being submitted to the Senate. A resolution in relation to them was passed and submitted to the Trustees, who have not taken any action upon it so far as I am aware. I do not remember any Professor, except the Plaintiff, Professors Lawson, Williamson and Dickson, expressing dissatisfaction with these Statutes. The action of the Senate in regard to these Statutes, was communicated to the Board of Trustees by me, as Secretary of the Senate. I received nothing in answer from the Board but a formal acknowledgment of receipt.

R

the (
to D
was
Leit
the
the
to th
tiff a
the
done
Seve
upon

fully,
and

Boar
bibit

Desc:

Febru
the C
latter

student
quentl
we ha
remov
in cor
be sho
was th
sapten
thing.
stated.
of Sup

Cross continued.—I was on intimate terms with the late Dr. Leitch. I was aware of the preparation by Dr. Leitch, of the statement read at the meeting of the ninth of February, 1861. At this time Dr. Leitch was generally confined to his bed by illness. This statement was submitted to the Board, I believe, because Dr. Leitch was too ill to make a statement in person. My belief was, that Plaintiff took every opportunity of thwarting Dr. Leitch' matters relating to the College. On one occasion, at a meeting of the Senatus, he exhibited strong personal hostility to Dr. Leitch. This was at the end of October, or beginning of November last. The Principal was accused of discourtesy by another Professor present, and Plaintiff said in presence of Dr. Leitch, it was to be attributed to his ignorance. About a year ago, at a meeting of Professors, the Plaintiff, in the absence of the Principal, spoke disrespectfully of him; others present did the same. I was aware that there was division among the students, and dissensions in regard to the state of feeling existing between the Plaintiff and Dr. Leitch, and also between the Plaintiff and Dr. George. I think they must have had a very distracting effect upon the studies of the students, and a very injurious effect upon their morals, resulting in many villanous things done by the students, consisting generally of manifestations of ill feeling towards the Principal. Several Trustees have spoken to me on the subject of Professor Weir's conduct, and its effect upon the welfare of the College.

Re-examined.—The meeting of the Professors at which Dr. Leitch was spoken of disrespectfully, was called to consider the Statutes. Many of the Professors strongly condemned them, and on that occasion blamed the Principal for them, and also found fault with him in other things.

(Signed.)   JOHN C. MURRAY.

I look at a paper, a copy of the proceedings of the Senate in relation to the Statutes of the Board. (Exhibit "W.") I also produce a memorandum found among Dr. Leitch's papers. (Exhibit "N.")

(Signed.)   JOHN C. MURRAY.

DUNCAN MORRISON, sworn:

I am one of the Trustees of Queen's College, and as such attended the meeting of the ninth February, 1861. I knew that the subject of the meeting was to consider the disturbances in the College, arising out of Professor ___'s conduct. That was my impression, as these disturbances were of public notoriety.

Cross-examined.—I have been a Trustee for upwards of five years. I had been previously a student in the College. I have been in the habit of attending meetings of the Board very frequently since I have been Trustee. I was at the meeting of the 8th May, 1862. We felt that we had not sufficient power granted to us by the Charter to procure evidence. I voted for the removal of Professor Weir, the Plaintiff, at the meeting of the 9th and 10th February, 1861, in consequence of his conduct to the Principal. I thought it for the interest of the College that he should be removed. Trustees stated of their own knowledge how injurious to the College was the Plaintiff's presence in it. I knew of students who would not attend the College in consequence of Plaintiff's connection with it. Several of the Trustees stated that they knew the same thing. Mr. Spence, of Ottawa, Mr. McLean, of Cornwall, Mr. Neilson, of Belleville, I think, so stated. Another cause for my vote against Plaintiff was, his rebellion to the Board in the matter of Superintendent of Common Schools. Plaintiff gave me to understand that he would not re-

;
i.
f
it
e:
h

te

At.

rea
evid
ceiv
mee
the
that
tiff.
spok
was
peop
view
such
Dr. L
and n
Leitel
oppor
though
read t
by him
as he
had to
way di
Staten
Plainti
of Plai
eral op
Local
taken,
Malloc
the mo
discuss
who di

sign his place as Superintendent, though I remonstrated with him against it. I considered him guilty of insubordination to the College authorities. I knew that there were strong hostile feelings between Dr. George and the Plaintiff. Prior to the trial of the Plaintiff in May, 1862, three or four of the Trustees communicated with Plaintiff with a view to make peace. Dr. Leitch thought it could be effected, and was very anxious to bring it about. The Plaintiff on this occasion exhibited, as I thought, though not in words, very hostile feelings towards Professor Leitch. I have seen the papers, or others similar to them (*Exhi it R and T.*)

Re-examined.—There was no desire expressed at the Board that Plaintiff should be called before the Board in relation to the charge of his acting as Local Superintendent of Schools.

(Signed.) DUNCAN MORRISON

ALEXANDER LOGIE, re-called :

I look at *Exhibit V.* It is in the handwriting of Dr. Leitch, and is, I think, the document read by me at the meeting of the 9th and 10th February, 1864, and referred to in my former evidence. About a week or ten days, I think, before the meeting of the 9th February, 1864, I received the circular calling the meeting. This was the first, and only intimation I received of the meeting and its objects, before I reached Kingston from Hamilton where I reside. On the day of the meeting I met at Dr. Leitch's, Mr. Paton, Mr. Morris, and Dr. Urquhart, I think. I was, on that occasion, informed by Dr. Leitch of some circumstances relating to the conduct of the Plaintiff. I think Dr. Mathieson was present when I heard these. The question of Plaintiff's dismissal was spoken of ; introduced, I think, by Dr. Leitch. The power of the Trustees to dismiss at pleasure was discussed. Dr. Leitch said he would be present, if possible, and read a statement he had prepared, but if unable to do so, he would give it to some Trustee to read for him. Dr. Leitch's view was, that there should be no delay in dealing with Mr. Weir, as the College had got into such a state, in consequence of his conduct, that it would be impossible to carry it on. I think Dr. Leitch desired either a summary dismissal, or summary trial of the Plaintiff. Mr. Morris and myself were of opinion that there should be a summary trial, not summary dismissal. Dr. Leitch objected to any delay. He required immediate action, which would not have afforded opportunity for a trial, if charges were to be made and answered, as Mr. Morris and myself thought should be done. Dr. Leitch handed to me, in his room, the written statement which I read to the Board, and with a request that I would read it for him in lieu of a verbal statement by him. I stated to the meeting that this written statement was to be returned to Dr. Leitch, as he wished it to be received merely as his verbal statement, and to be returned to him, as he had told me to do on entrusting it to me, I had no authority to leave it with the Board. There was discussion at the meeting on the subject of this statement. No witnesses were called in.— Statements of facts were made by some of the Trustees, such as their knowledge of the fact that Plaintiff had accepted the office of Superintendent of Common Schools, and that in consequence of Plaintiff's conduct, young men had been deterred from coming to College. I think the general opinion of the Trustees was, that the resolution of the Board in regard to the Plaintiff being Local Superintendent, taken in connection with the Statutes, was mandatory, but no vote was taken, and it was not of itself considered a sufficient cause for action against Plaintiff. Judge Malloch, Mr. Morris, and myself, thought Plaintiff ought to have notice, and have a trial. On the morning of the 10th February, on the resolution dismissing Plaintiff, there was considerable discussion. A number of the Trustees expressed their opinion. I think there were very few who did not do so. A great many of the Trustees, on the evening before, stated that they knew

tl:za
Lite
ary, I
meeti
nging
I tho
Board
Camp
they e

JAMES

I
Univer
Cook,
sities.
ularly
agreea

Jons I

I
last da
Februa
referre
tion an
Dr. La
resigna
respect

Co
their fo
College
where a

that many of the charges against Plaintiff, contained in Dr. Leitch's written statement read by me, were true. I thought, as did Mr. Morris, that we had power to dismiss summarily, but that a trial was the preferable course. No witness in support of Dr. Leitch's statement, was produced or called for. The Board removed the Plaintiff in consequence of his general conduct throughout, and particularly after he had been admonished by the resolution of May, 1862. The Board asserted, and exercised the right to remove at discretion.

Cross-examined.—I was at the meeting of the 8th May, 1862. Several of the witnesses refused to answer questions put to them at the meeting. We had no power to compel them, and thus could not get at the truth, and the investigation was therefore not effectual. Principal Leitch spoke strongly in favour of Mr. Weir on this occasion. At the meeting of the 9th February, 1861, allusion was made to the ineffectual efforts of the Board to extract evidence at the meeting of May, 1862. The difficulties which have existed in the College have had a very damaging effect upon its prosperity. I allude to the difficulties in which the Plaintiff was concerned. I thought it for the interest of the College that the Plaintiff should be removed, and that the Board had the power of removing him at discretion. The legal opinion of the Honourable Mr. Campbell had been obtained for the guidance of the Board, and on it they acted; that is, that they could remove the Plaintiff without cause, if they thought it advisable to do so.

(Signed.)   A. LOGIE.

JAMES WILLIAMSON, sworn as a witness:

I have been a Professor in Queen's College for several years. I am a Master of Arts in the University of Edinburgh, and Doctor of Laws in the University of Glasgow. I agree with Dr. Cook, a witness here, as to the notion of the tenure of office of Professors in the Scotch Universities. I disapproved of some of the Statutes of the College, which have been referred to, particularly those relating to the tenure of office of Professors. I have found the Plaintiff a very agreeable person to deal with in the College.

(Signed.)   JAMES WILLIAMSON.

JOHN ROBINSON DICKSON, sworn:

I was a Professor in the Medical Faculty of Queen's College from its establishment till the last day of March, 1861, my resignation to take effect then, having been sent in on the 15th of February previously. The cause of this was the Statutes of the College, which have been referred to as stated by me in my letter of resignation. These Statutes gave general dissatisfaction among the Professors of the College, and this spirit of dissatisfaction reached the students. Dr. Lawson resigned for the same cause. In addresses to him and myself, on our respective resignation, the students expressed the strongest dissatisfaction with the action of the Board in respect of these Statutes.

Cross-examined.—When Dr. Lawson was about resigning, I told the students that whatever their feelings might be in regard to Dr. Leitch, they should express them for the good of the College. I condemned to them the conduct of the Trustees. This was in the Convocation Room, where an address was being presented to Dr. Lawson by the students.

(Signed.)   JOHN R. DICKSON.

lan
to t
the
fron
ease
nile

not
recei
and t

WILLIAM MAXWELL INGLIS, sworn :

I am one of the Trustees of Queen's College. I am a Graduate of the University of Edinburgh. I am of opinion that the tenure of office of Professors in the Scotch Universities, prior to the recent Imperial Act, was for life. There can be no doubt this was so. I was present at the meeting of the 9th February, 1861. I had letters from some of the Trustees. I have had letters from Mr. Morris, of Montreal. Before the meeting of the 9th February I had heard that the case of Plaintiff would come before the meeting, but I can't tell how I heard it. There was much public talk about the case.

Cross-examined.—I did not vote at the meeting of the 9th and 10th February, because I had not before me sufficient data on which to base a judgment. I have no recollection of having received a letter from Mr. Morris, stating that they were going to have a meeting of Trustees and to dismiss the Plaintiff, nor have I ever stated so to the Plaintiff. The Plaintiff must have misunderstood me if he says I did so state.

(Signed.)   WM. MAXWELL INGLIS.

WILLIAM IRELAND, sworn.

I produce letters of Plaintiff to Dr. George, relating to charges made by former against latter, in 1861. (Exhibits AA, BB, CC, DD, EE, FF, GG, HH, II.) A resolution of the Board of 2nd December, 1844, refers to the right of the College to the Commutation Fund. The Minute Book No. 2 is the authorized record of the proceedings of the Board of Trustees.

(Signed.)   W. IRELAND.

WITNESSES FOR DEFENCE.

MICHAEL LAVELL, sworn :

I am a Medical Professor and a member of the Governing Board of Victoria College. I am acquainted with the tenure of Professorships in Victoria College. It has a Royal Charter.

(Signed.)   M. LAVELL

JOHN PATON, sworn.—Called as a witness for co-defendants.

I have been a Trustee for several years, and have been connected with the College since 1851. There was a dissatisfaction between Plaintiff and Professor Smith shortly after I became connected with the College. I have heard Plaintiff speak slightingly of Professor Smith. This disagreement was, I think, prejudicial to the College. I brought forward charges against the Plaintiff at the meeting of the 8th May, 1862. I was unable to sustain some of them because we could not compel the giving of evidence. I am not aware of any pre-conceived plan among the Trustees, or any of them, to remove the Plaintiff prior to the meeting of the 9th February,

1861, and I don't think there was any, though I believe many of the Trustees had already formed the opinion that the interests of the College required his removal. The discussions at the meeting were calm and deliberate, and continued till twelve o'clock on the night of the 9th. The effect of Professor Weir's conduct in the College was injurious, and calculated to mar its influence. It gave rise to two factions in the College, one of which known as Plaintiff's was constantly abusing the Principal. The resolution against Plaintiff holding office of Superintendent of Schools, was based on the Statutes of the College, and so considered mandatory, and I considered the Plaintiff guilty of contumacy in retaining the place. Many of the Professors took opposing sides in the matter of these difficulties.

Cross-examined.—The disagreement between Plaintiff and Professor Smith was observed by me soon after I joined the institution. Smith was drowned four or five years ago. This dispute was the first of a series which created the troubles which brought about the removal of the Plaintiff. I considered that the decision of the Board of 8th May, 1862, delivered the Plaintiff from the charges disposed of thereby, in case he in the future conducted himself in a proper manner. In voting for the removal of Plaintiff, I was influenced by his conduct both before and after the 8th May, 1862. I knew the object for which the meeting of the 9th February last, was called. Just before the issuing of the notice calling the meeting, Dr. Leitch told me he had a communication to make to the Board regarding Plaintiff. The Plaintiff's conduct was repeatedly the subject of conversation between Dr. Leitch and myself. Before the meeting Dr. Leitch told me that, in his opinion, the Plaintiff ought to be dismissed. I saw the opinion of Mr. Campbell as to the power of the Trustees to remove Professors prior to the meeting of the 9th February. Dr. Leitch, I believe, procured that opinion. He expressed a wish to have Mr. Campbell's opinion. I thought that Professor Weir should have been dismissed in May, 1862; and I have thought so up to the present time. There have been difficulties in the College arising out of the conduct of other Professors than the Plaintiff. I believe that the understanding of the Statutes by the Professors created dissatisfaction in some of them. I believe this tended to diminish the good working of the institution, and communicated itself to the students who were divided in opinion on the subject. I believe some of the Professors sympathized with Plaintiff. It was understood that the Statutes were not to affect the tenure of office of existing officers. At the meeting of the 9th February, Judge Malloch urged that Plaintiff should have a trial. I considered that charges had been duly proved against Plaintiff under the provisions of the Charter. I was actuated by the Plaintiff's conduct generally. I was partly acting under the inherent power which I considered the Board to possess, to remove without cause.

(Signed,   JOHN PATON

JOHN B. MOWAT, sworn :

I have been a Professor in Queen's College since 1857, and have been in the habit of attending meetings of the Senatus, and have observed the conduct of Plaintiff there to Principal Leitch. I thought his tone and manner to the Principal offensive, and that it was intentionally so. This occurred in the presence of other Professors.

Cross-examined.—This manner of the Plaintiff was exhibited in discussions in the Senatus on the business of the College. His language was warm, but it was principally his tone and manner that were objectionable. On one occasion, in the presence of the Principal, a Professor complained that the Principal was in the habit of sending messages to Plaintiff to converse on

other
disco
them

JAMES

I
March
studie
subjec
way o
had fir
class w
anothe
tiff, th
discuss
sion, P
He me
the stu
an add

Descr

I v
class,
told th
only w
was hei
was ad
student
only a
house.
ence of
Profess

Cv
signatu
signed
from it.

meeting written on the back of an envelope. Plaintiff said this was so, but that he attributed it to the ignorance of the Principal. This was in October or November last. I remember no other offensive language of the Plaintiff. The Professor who had complained of this, thought it discourteous to the Principal. The Statutes were objected to, and the discussions in regard to them warm.

(Signed,)   J. H. MOWAT.

JAMES B. FERGUSON, sworn:

I was a student of Queen's College, in Arts, in the Session of 1862-63, and 1861-62. In March of 1862, I remember the Plaintiff addressing his class on subjects not relating to their studies. He read portions of two letters which he said he had received from Trustees on the subject of his dispute with Dr. George. He said he did not wish to influence the students one way or another in the matter, but that he wished to clear his own character. It was after he had finished the lecture to his class that this occurred. On this a meeting of the students of his class was held, and the subject of it discussed among them. Some taking one side, and some another. Two parties were formed among the students of this class, one party supporting Plaintiff, the other Dr. George. Feeling, in consequence of this, ran high among the students, who discussed the conduct of the Trustees, some speaking disrespectfully of them. On another occasion, Plaintiff again referred to his dispute with Dr. George, when the students were present.— He merely alluded to the subject, saying that a petition in relation to it, sent to the Senatus by the students, had not been granted, and that he was sorry for it. At this meeting of students an address was adopted praying that Dr. George might not be continued as examiner.

(Signed,)   JAMES B. FERGUSON.

DUNCAN MORRISON, the younger, sworn:

I was a student of Queen's College in the Session of 1861 and '62, and in Professor Weir's class. I remember the occurrence spoken of by the last witness. The Plaintiff on that occasion told the students that if Dr. George took any part in the examination he would not. He said he only wished to clear his own character, and not to injure Dr. George. A meeting of the students was held immediately after this, and again a couple of meetings, the result being that an address was adopted to the Senatus, and sent to it. There was a good deal of discussion among the students on the subject of the disputes between Plaintiff and Dr. George. In fact it was the only subject talked of when the students assembled. Plaintiff asked me one night to his house. He and Mrs. Weir spoke to me on the subject, one or other of them saying in the presence of the other, that it was a disgrace that such an immoral man as Dr. George should be a Professor of Morality.

Cross-examined.—I remember a paper condoling with Dr. George being carried round for signature. I signed it. I think this was before Plaintiff mentioned the subject to his class. I also signed the address to the Senatus against Dr. George, but I afterwards withdrew my name from it.

(Signed,)   DUN. MORRISON.

JAMES R. MULLEN, sworn :

I was a student in Queen's College commencing in 1856-'57, and continuing till the end of the Session of 1861-'62. I attended the classes of the Plaintiff and Dr. George. The disputes between Dr. George and Plaintiff gave rise to discussions among the students, who ranged themselves into two parties, one favouring Plaintiff, the other Dr. George.

Signed,   J. R. MULLEN

JOHN CORMACK, sworn :

I am janitor of the College, and have been so since July, 1861. I am in constant contact with the students. I remember the quarrel between Plaintiff and Dr. George, in 1861. The students were in the habit of discussing it warmly, taking different sides; the Plaintiff's party would pour abuse on Dr. George. During this last Session the students favouring the Plaintiff abused the Trustees and the Principal on the subject of the Statutes of the College, which have been spoken of.

Cross-examined.—I knew the leading supporters of Plaintiff among the students. I would hear them speak in favour of Plaintiff and abuse the Principal. The majority of students of the College, including the Medical students among them, might have supported Plaintiff. On Dr. George's resignation the discussion in reference to his dispute with Plaintiff subsided. The Statutes and other things have since formed the subject of talk.

(Signed,)   JOHN CORMACK.

28th September, 1864.

JOHN PATON, recalled for Defendants :

I am Treasurer of Queen's College. The Chair of Classical Literature is not specially endowed. It is paid out of the general revenues of the College, which are, to some extent, uncertain, as, for instance, the annual grants voted by the Legislature and the Colonial Committee of the Church of Scotland. The one hitherto has been $5,000 to the College and $800 to the Medical Faculty, and the other gives £300 sterling per annum. The investments of the College do not always produce the same sum yearly. The College is also dependent on voluntary contributions to some extent.

Cross-examined.—The excuse this year will not depend on voluntary contributions. The voluntary contributions which are received, are, and are to be invested, and from these investments additional revenue is expected. I was in error yesterday in stating that Professor Smith was drowned. He died from the effects of bathing.

(Signed,)   JOHN PATON.

HORATIO YATES, sworn :

I am the Dean of the Medical Faculty of Queen's College. I have been a member of the Faculty for ten years past. I was the medical attendant of Dr. Leitch in his last illness from which he died. I thought his illness aggravated by mental anxiety. I think he suffered much from the difficulties with the Plaintiff. I have been present at meetings of the Senatus when

both Plaintiff and Dr. Leitch were present. I think the disputes between Plaintiff and Dr. George had a disturbing influence on the mind and conduct of the students, or of some of them. At the time of the meeting of the 9th and 10th. February last, Dr. Leitch was dangerously ill.

(Signed,)   HORATIO YATES.

THE PLAINTIFF examined as a party :

I have seen the pamphlet marked exhibit T, and I have seen the manuscript of it. I do not know who was the author of it, or any portion of it. I do not know that my wife was the author of it. She never told me that she was. I have seen exhibit R. I have seen the manuscript of it. I am the author of some of the remarks appearing in it. I furnished the manuscript to Mr. Creighton, printer. I did not circulate the printed copies. I had them printed to rebut the false statements against me, intending to show them. I met Dr. Leitch cordially in Senate up to the time of my dismissal. I am not aware of having ever used disrespectful language to the Principal. I did not take legal proceedings against Dr. George for the seduction of my sister, as I was informed it was too late. My sister went home to Scotland in the fall of 1854. I knew the tenure of office of Professors in Scotch Universities before I accepted office in Queen's College. A letter signed by Mr. Paton, enclosing money, was brought me by a Mr. Drummond. I returned it at once.

(Signed.)   GEORGE WEIR.

JOHN C. MURRAY, re-called for Plaintiff :

I produce letters from Mr. Morris, Defendant, to Dr. Leitch (*Exhibits* 1 *M*, 2 *M*, 3 *M*, 4 *M*,) also letter from Mr. Paton to Dr. Leitch (*Exhibit* 5 *M*), also another letter from Mr. Morris (*Exhibit* 6 *M*), also a letter from Chief Justice McLean (*Exhibit* 7 *M*), also a letter from Defendant, John Hamilton, (*Exhibit* 8 *M*,) also memorandum in handwriting of Dr. Leitch, (*Exhibits* 9 *M and* 10 *M*,) also a letter from Chief Justice McLean, and form of summons, (*Exhibits* 11 *M and* 12 *M*,) also a letter from Mr. Morris to Dr. Leitch, with memorandum enclosed, (*Exhibits* 13 *M and* 14 *M*.)

(Signed,)   JOHN C. MURRAY.

JAMES WILLIAMSON, re-called for Plaintiff :

I produce the documents (*Exhibits* L, L and M M) referred to in the report of the Committee on the subject of the appropriation of the Commutation fund claimed by College.

(Signed,)   JAMES WILLIAMSON.

IN REBUTTAL BY PLAINTIFF.

CLUSTON KELLY, sworn :

I was a student of Queen's College during the Session of 1863-64. There was a large meeting of students on one occasion in the hall of the College, when an address to Plaintiff was adopted by a large majority of those present. There was much dissatisfaction among the students on the subject of the Statutes. I never heard Plaintiff's name mentioned in connection with them till after his removal from the College.

10

Cross-examined.—I have read the Statutes. I did not know that the Professors then in office were not effected by them.

(Signed,)   C. W. KELLY.

JAMES WYLIE, sworn :

I was a student of Queen's College during the Sessions of 1862-63, and 1863-64. The students were dissatisfied with the footing on which dismissal of the Professors was placed. There was no misunderstanding among the students that I am aware of. There were two or three meetings of the students in regard to Plaintiff. An address to Plaintiff was ultimately adopted by the greater portion of the students then attending College. I look at this address which was presented to Plaintiff, (*Exhibit N N.*) I suppose there were one hundred and fifty students attending College at the time.

Cross-examined.—I have heard Plaintiff find fault with Dr. Leitch's acts.

(Signed,)   JAMES WYLIE.

DOCUMENTS PRODUCED BY PLAINTIFF under order for production:—

I.

Letter from Dr. COOK to PROFESSOR MENZIES, dated 25th July, 1853.

DEAR SIR,—

I think I may venture to ask you to do a favor to our Canadian College. The enclosed copy of a minute of the Board of Trustees will explain what it is. When in Scotland, my impression was, that Geddes was the most accomplished scholar, Weir the most amiable and attractive man. We shall be satisfied with your choice between the two, if we may have choice, or if both refuse, with any one you appoint, having entire confidence in your judgment. I may mention that the salary is £350 a year cy., equal to £290 sterling, and that it will go as far here as £35 sterling at home. No fees. It is desirable that whoever comes should be in the field early in October.

I am hastening to the seaside, and have only time to catch the mail. I fear you must lay the blame of this trouble on me, but hoping you will excuse it,

I am, &c.,

Yours truly,

JOHN COOK.

II.

Letter from ALLAN MENZIES to Plaintiff, dated 15 Aug., 1853.

MY DEAR SIR,—

In consequence of a letter from Dr. Cook, Quebec, I have written to Mr. Geddes about the Professorship in Queen's College. It is possible, however, Mr. Geddes having recently been

appointed Rector of the Grammar School, that he may not now be disposed to go to Canada, and my purpose in writing to you at present is to enquire whether you are still of the mind to go, should Mr. Geddes decline. Please let me know by return of post, and if Mr. Geddes declines, I shall send you the particulars which Dr. Cook has furnished. It is wished that the Professor be in the field early in October.

I remain, &c.,

ALLAN MENZIES.

Mr. Weir, Rector Grammar School, Banff.

III.

Letter from PROFESSOR MENZIES *to Plaintiff, dated 22nd Aug., 1853.*

MY DEAR SIR,—

I received your letter of the 16th inst., but have only this morning heard from Mr. Geddes, declining the appointment. The whole particulars furnished by Dr. Cook are contained in the following paragraph from his letter : " I may mention that the salary is £350 a year cur- " rency, equal to £300 sterling, and that it will go as far here as £350 sterling at home. No fees. " It is desirable that whoever comes should be in the field early in October."

It is evident that in such a matter you must be decided by your own views and feelings. If you feel a call to the ministry, this, I should think, would be an impediment in following that out ; but the matter, altogether, as I have said, must be with yourself.

I would be glad to hear from you on or before Thursday, in order that by Friday's despatch from this I may be able to give Dr. Cook an idea as to the probability of your going. On the other hand, should you decline, it will be highly necessary to be making enquiries in other quar- ters with as little delay as possible.

I remain, &c.,

(Sd.,)   ALLAN MENZIES.

Mr. Weir, &c.

IV.

Letter from PROFESSOR MENZIES *to Plaintiff, dated 10th Sept., 1853.*

DEAR SIR,—

I have this morning received your note of the 8th inst. My letter of 22nd ultimo contained, as I mentioned, the whole particulars given by Dr. Cook. For your perfect satisfac- tion, however, I now enclose his letter to me of 25th July last, with relative enclosure, which is the only communication that I have received from Dr. Cook. Although the information is meagre, still, having implicit confidence in Dr. Cook, it is my impression that you ought to go without hearing again from him, there being, in fact, no time to receive a reply from him before the period at which he says you ought to be in Canada, my letter announcing your acceptance having been despatched on the 25th ultimo.

If you cannot depart earlier than the 6th October, you ought to lose no time in writing to Dr. Cook (his address is Quebec), apprising him of the fact.

accu
sel w
may

\

the 2(

It
unani

T
in proc
E:

Victor

To all te

I. W'
America
of the (
Literatu

42

I heard lately that there are now steam packets from Liverpool to the St. Lawrence direct. You had better enquire about that, as you would thus be saved both time and expense probably. If you are in Edinburgh before your departure, we shall rely upon seeing you at Murrayfield.

Yours, &c.,

(Sd.,) ALLAN MENZIES.

Mr. Weir, Academy, Banff.

V.

Letter from Professor Menzies *to Plaintiff, dated 29th Sept., 1853.*

MY DEAR SIR,—

I have received a letter from Dr. Cook, expressing much satisfaction that you have accepted the appointment, and he states that he thinks you might sail from Liverpool by a vessel which would land you at Quebec, so that you would see him on your way to Kingston. This may be worthy your consideration, if your plans are not irreversibly fixed.

Shan't we see you in Edinburgh before you sail.

Yours sincerely,

(Sd.,) ALLAN MENZIES.

VI.

At a meeting of the Board of Trustees of Queen's College, held in Kingston, on Wednesday, the 20th day of July, 1853:

Inter Alia.

It was moved by the Honourable Peter McGill, seconded by Hugh Allan, Esquire, and unanimously resolved,—

That the thanks of the Board be given to the Reverend Dr. Cook for his valuable services in proceeding to Scotland for the purpose of procuring Professors for this University.

Extracted from the minutes of the meeting by

W. McIVER,
Secretary to the Board of Trustees of Queen's College, Kingston.

VII.

Royal Charter of QUEEN'S COLLEGE, KINGSTON, *dated 16th October, 1841.*

VICTORIA, BY THE GRACE OF GOD OF THE UNITED KINGDOM OF GREAT BRITAIN AND IRELAND, QUEEN, DEFENDER OF THE FAITH:

To all to whom these Presents shall come, Greeting:

I. *Whereas,* the establishment of a College within the Province of Upper Canada, in North America, in connection with the Church of Scotland, for the education of youth in the principles of the Christian Religion; and for their instruction in the various branches of Science and Literature, would greatly conduce to the welfare of our said Province. *And Whereas* humble

or u
Chu
full
and
STO

HI
Heir
them
their
style
Aris
chang
and th
in Eq
and he
acquir
Messan
that th
and ni
enjoy,
Contri
demise,
sound,
best for

IV.
to be n

43

application hath been made to us by THE REVD. ROBERT McGILL, Moderator of the Synod of the Presbyterian Church of Canada in connection with the Church of Scotland, and THE REVD. ALEXANDER GALE, Clerk of the said Synod, and the several other persons hereinafter named, to make them a Body Corporate and Politic for the purposes aforesaid and hereinafter mentioned ; by granting to them our Royal Charter of Incorporation, and to permit them to use our Royal Title in the name or style thereof.

II. *Now know Ye*, that We having taken the premises into our Royal consideration, and duly weighing the great utility and importance of such an Institution, have of our special grace, certain knowledge, and mere motion, granted, constituted, declared and appointed, and by these Presents for Us, Our Heirs and Successors, Do grant, constitute, declare and appoint the said ROBERT McGILL and ALEXANDER GALE, The Revd. JOHN McKENZIE, The Revd. WILLIAM RINTOUL, The Revd. WILLIAM T. LEACH, The Revd. JAMES GEORGE, The Revd. JOHN MACHAR, The Revd. PETER COLIN CAMPBELL, The Revd. JOHN CRUIKSHANK, The Revd. ALEXANDER MATHIESON, Doctor in Divinity, The Revd. JOHN COOK, Doctor in Divinity, and the PRINCIPAL of the said College for the time being, Ministers of the Presbyterian Church of Canada in connection with the Church of Scotland, The Honorable JOHN HAMILTON, The Honorable JAMES CROOKS, The Honorable WM. MORRIS, The Honorable ARCHIBALD McLEAN, The Honorable JOHN McDONALD, The Honorable PETER McGILL, EDWARD W. THOMSON, THOMAS McKAY, JAMES MORRIS, JOHN EWART, JOHN STEELE, JOHN MOWAT, ALEXANDER PRINGLE, JOHN MUNN and JOHN STRANG, Esquires, Members of the said Church, and all and every other such person and persons as now is or are, or shall or may at any or times hereafter be Ministers of the Presbyterian Church of Canada in connection with the Church of Scotland—or Members of the said Presbyterian Church in such connection, and in full communion with the said Presbyterian Church—shall be and be called, one body Corporate and Politic, in Deed and in Law by the name and style of "QUEEN'S COLLEGE AT KINGSTON," and them by the name of " QUEEN'S COLLEGE AT KINGSTON."

III. *We do for* the purposes aforesaid and hereinafter mentioned, really and fully for Us, Our Heirs and Successors, make, erect, create, ordain, constitute, establish, confirm and declare by these presents, to be one Body Politic and Corporate in Deed and in name : And that they and their Successors by that name shall and may have perpetual succession as a College—with the style and privileges of an University, for the education and instruction of Youth and Students in Arts and faculties ; and shall also have and may use a Common Seal, with power to break, change, alter or make new the same Seal, as often as they shall judge expedient. And that they and their Successors, by the name aforesaid, shall and may forever hereafter be able, in Law and in Equity, to sue and be sued, implead and be impleaded, answer and be answered unto, defend and be defended, in all Courts and places whatsoever : and also to have, take, receive, purchase, acquire, hold, possess, enjoy and maintain in Law, to and for the use of the said College, any Messuages, Lands, Tenements and Hereditaments, of what kind, nature or quality soever, so as that the same do not exceed in yearly value, above all charges, the sum of £15,000 Sterling : and also that they and their Successors shall have power to take, purchase, acquire, have, hold, enjoy, receive, possess and retain all or any Goods, Chattels, Monies, Stocks, Charitable or other Contributions, Gifts, Benefactions or Bequests whatsoever : and to give, grant, bargain, sell, demise, or otherwise dispose of, all or any part of the same : or of any other property, real, personal, or other they may at any time or times possess or be entitled to, as to them shall seem best for the interest of the said College.

IV. *And We do further Will*, Ordain and Grant, that the said College shall be deemed and taken to be an University ; and that the Students in the said College shall have liberty and faculty of .

11

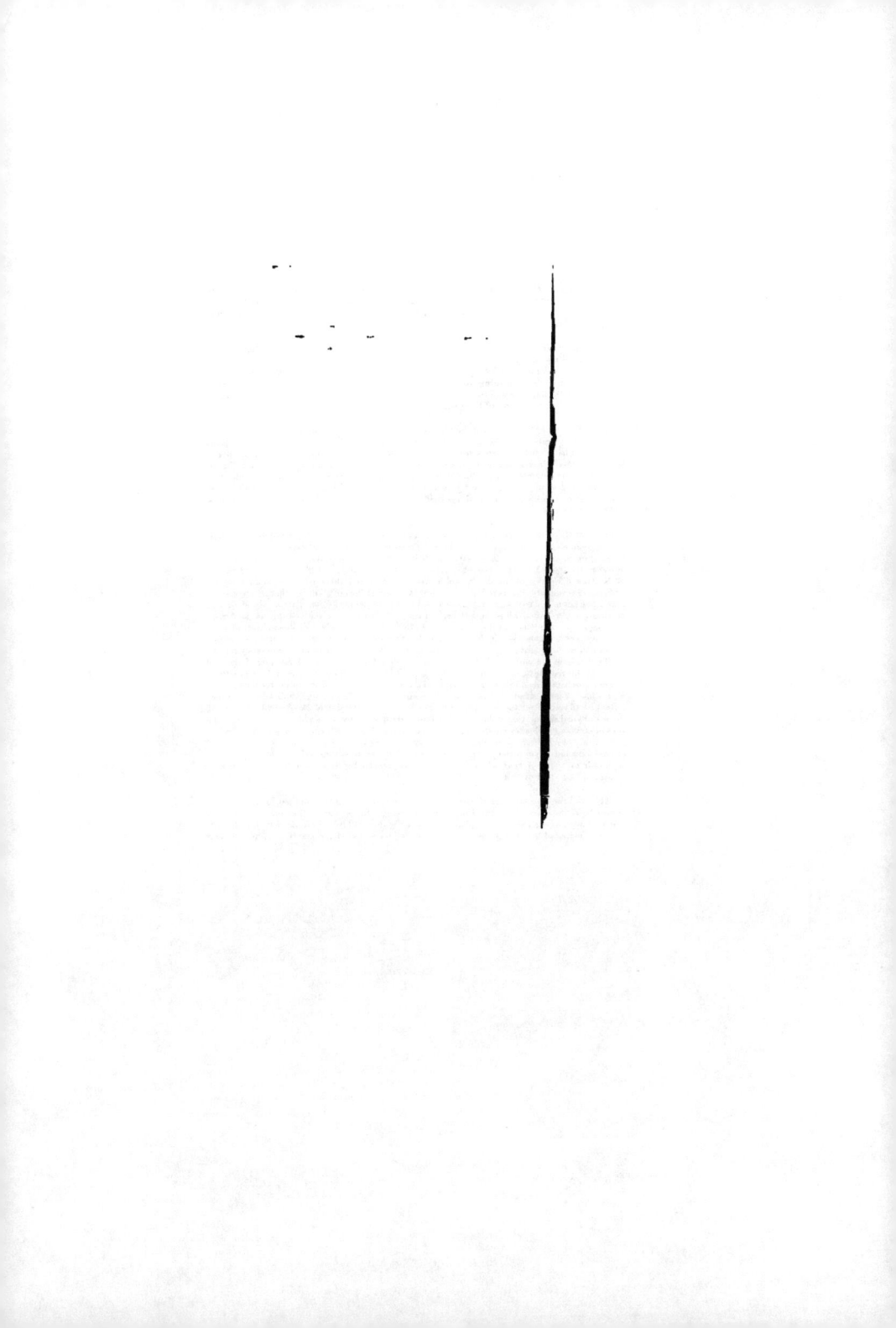

44

taking the degrees of Bachelor, Master and Doctor in the several Arts and faculties at the appointed times; and shall have liberty within themselves of performing all Scholastic Exercises for conferring such Degrees, in such manner as shall be directed by the Statutes, Rules and Ordinances of the said College.

V. *And We do further Will*, Ordain and appoint that no religious test or qualification shall be required of, or appointed or any persons admitted or matriculated as Scholars within our said College; or of or for persons admitted to any Degree in any Art or Faculty therein, save only that all persons admitted within Our said College to any Degree of Divinity, shall make such and the same Declarations and Subscriptions as are required of persons admitted to any Degree of Divinity in Our University of Edinburgh.

VI. *And for the better execution* of the purposes aforesaid, and for the more regular Government of the said Corporation, We do declare and Grant that the said Corporation and their Successors shall forever have Twenty-seven Trustees, of whom Twelve shall be Ministers of the said Presbyterian Church of Canada, and Fifteen shall be Laymen in full communion with the said Church. And that the said several persons hereinbefore named and the Principal of the said College for the time being, shall be the first and present Trustees of the said Corporation, and shall respectively continue in such Office until others shall be appointed in their stead, in pursuance of these our Letters Patent.

VII. *And We further Will* that the said Trustees, of the said Corporation hereinbefore particularly named, shall continue in and hold the office of Trustees until the several days and in the manner hereinafter mentioned, that is to say, three Ministers and four Laymen whose names stand lowest in these our Letters Patent, shall retire from the said Board of Trustees on the first day of the Annual Meeting of the said Synod in the year 1843, and their room be supplied by the addition of seven new Members in manner hereinafter mentioned. Three other Ministers and four other Laymen whose names stand next to those in these our Letters Patent, who shall have previously retired, shall retire from the said Board of Trustees on the first day of the Annual Meeting of the said Synod in the year 1844, and their room be supplied by the addition of seven new members in manner hereinafter mentioned. Three other Ministers and four other Laymen whose names stand next to those in these our Letters Patent who shall have previously retired, shall retire from the said Board of Trustees on the first day of the Annual Meeting of the said Synod in the year 1845, and their room be supplied by the addition of seven new Members in manner hereinafter mentioned; and the two remaining Ministers and the three remaining Laymen whose names stand next to those in these our Letters Patent, who shall have previously retired, shall retire from the said Board of Trustees on the first day of the Annual Meeting of the said Synod in the year 1846, and their room be supplied by the addition of five new Members in manner hereinafter mentioned. And on the first day of each succeeding Annual Meeting of the said Synod, three ministers and four Laymen whose names stand lowest in the future roll of Ministers and Laymen composing the said Board of Trustees, shall retire from the same, excepting in every fourth year, when two Ministers only, instead of three, and three Laymen only instead of four, shall so retire.

VIII. And the new Members of the Board to be appointed from time to time in succession to those who retire, shall be appointed in manner following, that is to say: The three Ministers or two Ministers, as the case may be, shall be chosen by the said Synod on the first day of every Annual Meeting of the same, in such manner as shall seem best to the said Synod; and the four

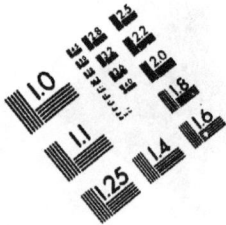

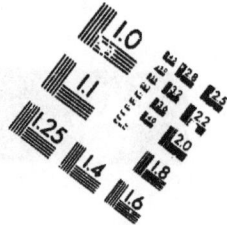

**IMAGE EVALUATION
TEST TARGET (MT-3)**

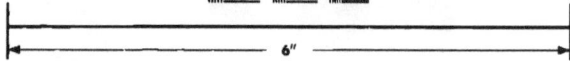

6"

Photographic
Sciences
Corporation

23 WEST MAIN STREET
WEBSTER, N.Y. 14580
(716) 872-4503

Laymen or three Laymen, as the case may be, shall be chosen also on the first day of every Annual Meeting of the said Synod, by the Lay Trustees remaining; after the others shall have retired ; and shall be so chosen from a list of persons made up in the following manner, that is to say : each Congregation admitted on the Roll of the said Synod, and in regular connection therewith, shall, at a meeting to be specially called from the Pulpit for that purpose in every third year, nominate one fit and discreet person, being a Member in full communion with the said Church, as eligible to fill the office of Trustee of the said College : and the persons names so nominated being duly intimated by the several Congregations to the Secretary of the Board of Trustees in such form as the said Board may direct, shall be enrolled by the said Board, and constitute the list from which Lay Trustees shall be chosen to fill the vacancies occurring at the Board during each year. And the names of Members thus added to the Board of Trustees, shall be placed from time to time at the top of the roll of the Board, the names of the Ministers chosen as new Trustees being first placed there in such order as the said Synod shall direct. And the names of the Laymen chosen as new Trustees being placed in such order as their Electors shall direct, immediately after the names of the said Ministers.

IX. *Provided always* that the retiring Trustees may be re-elected as heretofore provided, if the Synod and remaining Lay Trustees respectively see fit to do so.

X. *And Provided always,* that in case no election of new Trustees shall be made on the said first day of the Annual Meeting of the said Synod, then and in such case the said retiring Members shall remain in Office until their successors are appointed at some subsequent period.

XI. *And Provided always* that every Trustee, whether Minister or Layman, before entering on his duties as a Member of the said Board, shall have solemnly declared his belief of the Doctrines of the Westminster Confession of Faith, and his adherence to the Standards of the said Church in Government, Discipline and Worship ; and subscribed such a formula to this effect as may be prescribed by the said Synod ; and that such Declaration and Subscription shall in every case be recorded in the Books of the said Board.

XII. *And We further Will* that the said Trustees and their Successors shall forever have full power and authority to elect and appoint for the said College a Principal, who shall be a Minister of the Church of Scotland, or of the Presbyterian Church of Canada in connexion with the Church of Scotland ; and such Professor or Professors, Master or Masters, Tutor or Tutors, and such other Officer or Officers as to the said Trustees shall seem meet ; save and except only, that the first Principal of the said College, who is also to be Professor of Divinity, and likewise the first Professor of Morals in the said College, shall be nominated by the Committee of the General Assembly of the Church of Scotland.

XIII. Provided always that such person or persons as may be appointed to the Office of Principal or to any Professorship or other Office in the Theological department in the said College shall, before discharging any of the duties, or receiving any of the emoluments of such Office or Professorship, solemnly declare his belief of the doctrines of the Westminster Confession of Faith, and his adherence to the standards of the Church of Scotland, in government, discipline and worship, and subscribe such a formula to this effect as may be prescribed by the Synod of the Presbyterian Church of Canada, in connection with the Church of Scotland, and that such declaration and subscription be recorded in the Books of the Board of Trustees :

XV. .
Professo
of Trust
duly pre
may se

XVI.
recorde

XVII
and aut

XVII
di . t

XIX.
authori
governi
tures, 1
Profess
Stipeno
the nu
matter
said C:
renew,
shall s

XX.

XIV. And provided always, that such persons as shall be appointed to Professorships, not in the Theological Department in the said College, shall before discharging any of the duties, or receiving any of the emoluments of such Professorships, subscribe such a formula, declarative of their belief of the doctrines of the aforesaid Confession of Faith as the Synod may prescribe.

XV. *And We further Will*, that if any complaint respecting the conduct of the Principal, or any Professor, Master, Tutor, or other Officer of the said College, be at any time made to the Board of Trustees, they may institute an enquiry, and in the event of any impropriety of conduct being duly proved, they shall admonish, reprove, suspend, or remove the person offending, as to them may seem good—

XVI. Provided always, that the grounds of such admonition, reproof, suspension or removal be recorded at length in the Books of the said Board.

XVII. *And We further Will*, that the said Trustees and their successors shall have full power and authority to erect an Edifice or Edifices for the use of the said College—

XVIII. Provided always, that such Edifice or Edifices shall not be more than three miles distant from St. Andrew's Church in the Town of Kingston in the Province of Upper Canada.

XIX. *And We further Will*, that the said Trustees and their Successors shall have power and authority to frame and make Statutes, Rules and Ordinances touching and concerning the good government of the said College, the performance of Divine Service therein, the Studies, Lectures, Exercises, and all matters regarding the same; the number, residence and duties of the Professors thereof, the management of the revenues and property of the said College, the Salaries, Stipends provision and emoluments of and for the Professors, Officers and Servants thereof, the the number and duties of such Officers and Servants, and also touching and concerning any other matter or thing which to them shall seem necessary for the well being and advancement of the said College, and also from time to time by any new Statutes, rules or ordinances to revoke, renew, augment or alter, all, every, or any of the said Statutes, rules and ordinances as to them shall seem meet and expedient :

XX. Provided always, that the said Statutes, rules and ordinances, or any of them, shall not be repugnant to these presents, or to the Laws and Statutes of the said Province.

XXI. Provided also, that the said Statutes, rules and ordinances, in so far as they regard the performance of Divine Service in the said College, the duties of the Professors in the Theological Department thereof, and the Studies and exercises of the Students of Divinity therein, shall be subject to the inspection of the said Synod of the Presbyterian Church, and shall be forthwith transmitted to the Clerk of the said Synod, and be by him laid before the same at their next Meeting for their approval; and until such approval duly authenticated by the signatures of the Moderator and Clerk of the said Synod is obtained, the same shall not be in force.

XXII. *And We further Will*, that so soon as there shall be a Principal and one Professor in the said College, the Board of Trustees shall have authority to constitute under their Seal the said Principal and Professor, together with three members of the Board of Trustees, a Court to be called "The College Senate," for the exercise of Academical superintendence and discipline over the Students, and all other persons resident within the same, and with such powers for maintaining order and enforcing obedience to the Statutes, Rules and Ordinances of the said College, as to the said Board may seem meet and necessary :—

of 1
pur

X
time
Cha

X:
of th
resig
ment
a Lay
place
been
other
vaca

XX
at Ki
Pater
by the
writi
Provi

47

XXIII. Provided always, that so soon as three additional Professors shall be employed in the said College, no Trustee shall be a Member of the said College Senate, but that such Principal and all the Professors of the said College shall for ever constitute the College Senate, with the powers just mentioned.

XXIV. *And We further Will*, that whenever there shall be a Principal and four Professors employed in the said College, the College Senate shall have power and authority to confer the Degrees of Batchelor, Master, and Doctor, in the several Arts and Faculties.

XXV. *And We further Will*, that five of the said Trustees, lawfully convened as is hereinafter directed, shall be a quorum for the despatch of all business, except for the disposal and purchase of Real Estate, or for the choice or removal of the Principal or Professors, for any of which purposes there shall be a Meeting of at least thirteen Trustees.

XXVI. *And We further Will*, that the said Trustees shall have full power and authority, from time to time, to choose a Secretary and Treasurer; and also once in each year, or oftener, a Chairman who shall preside at all Meetings of the Board.

XXVII. *And We further Will*, that the said Trustees shall also have power, by a majority of voices of the Members present, to select and appoint, in the event of a vacancy in the Board by death, resignation, or removal from the Province, a person whose name is on the list from which appointments are to be made to fill such vacancy, choosing a Minister in the room of a Minister, and a Layman in the room of a Layman, and inserting the name of the person so chosen in that place on the Roll of the Board in which the name of the Trustee in whose stead he may have been chosen stood; so that the persons so chosen may be as to continuance in Office and in all other respects as the persons would have been by whose death, resignation or removal the vacancy was occasioned.

XXVIII. *And We further Will*, that the first General Meeting of the said Trustees shall be held at Kingston upon such a day within six Calendar months after the date of these our Letters Patent, as shall be fixed for that purpose by the Trustee first named in these presents, who shall be then living; of which Meeting, thirty days' notice at least shall be given by notification in writing to each of the Trustees for the time being, who shall be resident at the time within the Provinces of Upper or Lower Canada; and the same shall also be notified at the same time by Advertisement in one or more of the Public Newspapers of the said Provinces.

XXIX. And the said Trustees shall also afterwards have power to meet at Kingston aforesaid, or at such other place as they shall fix for that purpose upon their own adjournment, and likewise so often as they shall be summoned by the Chairman, or, in his absence, by the Senior Trustee, whose Seniority shall be determined in the first instance by the order in which the said Trustees are named in these presents, and afterwards by the order in which they shall be subsequently arranged pursuant to the powers hereinbefore contained.

XXX. Provided always, that the said Chairman or Senior Trustee shall not summon a Meeting of the Trustees unless required so to do by a notice in writing from three members of the Board :

XXXI. And provided also, that he cause notice of the time and place of the said Meeting to be given in one or more of the Public Newspapers of the Provinces of Upper and Lower Canada, at least thirty days before such Meeting ; and that every Member of the Board of Trustees resident

12

'Truste
cernin.
studies
duties
College
servant
concern
advanc

A:

Tl
at Kin
ton, Ch
Dunca
and A:
aforesc
for the

within the said Provinces shall be notified in writing by the Secretary to the Corporation of the time and place of such Meeting.

XXXII. *And We Will* and by these presents for Us, our Heirs and Successors, do Grant and declare that these our Letters Patent, or the enrolment or exemplification thereof shall and may be good, firm and valid, sufficient and effectual in the Law, according to the true intent and meaning of the same, and shall be taken, construed and adjudged in the most favourable and beneficial sense for the best advantage of our said College, as well in our Courts of Record as elsewhere ; and by all and singular Judges, Justices, Officers, Ministers, and others, subject whatsoever of Us, our Heirs and Successors, any unrecital, non-recital, omission, imperfection, defect, matter, cause, or anything whatsoever, to the contrary thereof in any wise notwithstanding.

In Witness Whereof, We have caused these our Letters to be made patent. Witness Ourself, at our Palace at Westminster, this Sixteenth day of October, in the Fifth year of our Reign.

By Writ of Privy Seal.—EDMUNDS.

VIII

Extracts from the Statutes, Rules and Ordinances of Queen's University and College.

PREAMBLE.

Whereas, the Charter of the University of "Queen's College, at Kingston," empowers the Trustees of the said College to frame and make Statutes, Rules and Ordinances, touching and concerning the good government of the said College ; the performance of Divine Service therein, the studies, lectures and exercises and all matters regarding the same ; the number, residence and duties of the professors thereof ; the management of the revenues and property of the said College ; the salaries, stipends, provisions and emoluments of and for the professors, officers and servants thereof ; the number and duties of such officers and servants ; and also touching and concerning any other matter or thing which to them shall seem necessary for the well-being and advancement of the said College ;

And whereas, it is necessary and expedient to make such Statutes, Rules and ordinances ;

Therefore, at a meeting of the Trustees of the said College, duly convened and holden, held at Kingston, on the 26th day of January, 1853, whereat there were present the Hon. John Hamilton,Chairman ; the Rev. Principal Leitch, the Rev. Dr. Williamson,the Rev. Dr. Urquhart, the Rev. Duncan Morrison, Alexander McLean, Hugh Allan, Alexander Morris, M. P. P.; John Paton and Andrew Drummond, Esquires, the said Trustees, by virtue of the power and authority as aforesaid vested in them, do enact, frame and make the following Statutes, Rules and Ordinances for the good government of the said College :

BOARD OF TRUSTEES.

10. All officers shall be appointed, shall have their duties prescribed by, and shall hold office only during the pleasure of the Trustees, except in cases where a special agreement may

I:
ho req
grean
Where
served

T
&c.,) i

V
Board
the sa
inquir
the So
your
requi
at the

have been or may be made ; and shall be entitled to such salaries or emoluments as may be from time to time agreed on.

12. The Trustees shall have the exclusive power of exercising discipline over the officers of the College.

13. Where a complaint is made respecting the conduct of any officer, the complainant shall be required to act as prosecutor, and, in the event of any impropriety being duly proved, the grounds of the sentence shall be recorded at length in the books of the Board of Trustees. Where the Board has resolved to institute an enquiry, a summons in the following form shall be served on the accused :—

To A. B———, of ———, in the City of Kingston, (Principal, Professor, or Janitor, &c.,) in Queen's College at Kingston :

Whereas a complaint hath been duly entered in writing against you, as such officer, before the Board of Trustees of the said College, of which a true copy is hereunto annexed ; and, whereas the said board hath resolved that the matter contained in the said complaint shall be further inquired into and adjudicated upon, you are, therefore, ' ' required to file, in the office of the Secretary of the said Board at the said College, w   after the service hereof, your answer to the matters in the said complaint conta   are hereby notified and required to be and appear in your proper person before   at a meeting to be held at the same College on ——— ———, the ——— ———. · next, in order to your defence in the said matter of complaint.

In witness whereof, the seal of the said College is hereto affixed.

(Signed),   ——————————— ,

Chairman Board of Trustees.

(Signed),   ——————————— ,

Secretary Board of Trustees.

14. The Trustees may, on their own motion, and without any complaint being made, deal with the Principal, Professors, Janitor, or any other officer, when they see cause. In such case it shall not be necessary that the grounds of censure, suspension or removal be recorded—the recording of the grounds being warranted only in the case of a judicial process in which a complainant acts as prosecutor. An officer on being removed shall be entitled to claim salary only up to the date of removal.

15. The Board of Trustees shall be a Court of Review and Appeal with respect to the decision of the College Senate, the Senatus, and all other College Boards.

THE PRINCIPAL.

21. He shall have the ordinary superintendence of the internal affairs of the College, under such regulations as the Board of Trustees may prescribe.

have

22. He shall, as chief executive officer, see that the laws of the College are carried out and observed by officers and students, and he shall employ such discretionary measures as may be necessary to secure this end without judicial procedure; but should it be necessary at any time to enforce the laws or exercise discipline, the case shall be laid before the Board of Trustees when relating to the officers of the College, and before the College Senate when relating to the students.

23. He shall from time to time inspect the Classes, Museum, Library, Minute Books, Matriculation Books, and Class Roll Books, and offer such suggestions to the officers as he may deem expedient; and should any department require the special attention of the Trustees, he shall report accordingly.

24. He shall, ex-officio, preside at the College Senate, and in the several faculty boards.

25. He shall preside at all examinations for degrees, and see that all examination papers are regularly set and valued.

26. He shall sign all diplomas for Degrees, Certificates of Honors awarded by the College Senate, and inspect all Certificates of Candidates for Degrees, and report to the Senate as to whether the requirements of the University have been complied with.

27. He shall sign all Minutes of Meetings of College Senate, and Senate; and should any meeting be held in his absence, the division of the meeting shall not be valid till the Minutes have received his signature or approval.

PROFESSORS.

31. They shall perform the duties of their office under such regulations as the Board of Trustees may from time to time prescribe, and shall not engage in any vocation which the Trustees shall deem inconsistent with their office.

IX.

Extract from Minutes of a Meeting of MEDICAL FACULTY OF QUEEN'S COLLEGE, *held in the College, 21st March, 1863. Present.*—DR. DICKSON, *Dean of the Faculty, in the Chair;* PROFESSORS H. YATES, FOWLER, LITCHFIELD, LAVELL, KENNEDY, *and* O. YATES.

The subject of the new Statutes, Rules, and Ordinances was taken up, and the following Deliverance was unanimously arrived at, a copy of which Deliverance the Dean was instructed to forward to the Board of Trustees, with a request that it should receive the attention of the Board at the first full meeting :—

MEMORANDUM.

The members of the Medical Faculty regret that the Board of Trustees should have passed By-Laws and Statutes for the government of said Faculty without consulting some of the members thereof.

the a

with
truts
rived
speci
to cal
2nd, :
at a r
exerci
emolu

"
Facult
as ma
purpos

Th
membe
grant, :
cal Fac

Th
all matt
have al
opinion
when th
are as e
the Sen
quently
of the :
would b
to restri
as past
sions for

In t
is offere
same tir

51

Rule 77 of said Statutes is antagonistic to certain resolutions passed by the Board of Trustees, both previous and subsequent to the establishment of the Medical School, and with an evident misunderstanding of the purpose for which the Government grant was first obtained, and the manner in which it is from year to year placed in the "Provincial Estimates."

There is not now, nor ever was, any sum granted by the Government to the *Trustees for the Medical Faculty*. The grant was given to the medical men of Kingston to assist them in establishing a "School of Medicine at Kingston," and to the said School of Medicine at Kingston the grant continues, from year to year, to be voted.

When the Medical Faculty was first formed, the Trustees undertook to furnish the Professors with suitable rooms in which to conduct their lectures, and to supply them with apparatus to illustrate their respective branches, and agreed that "the emoluments of the Professors should be derived from the fees of the Students, and any funds which might hereafter be obtained for the special endowment of a School of Medicine." In proof of which the Medical Faculty begs leave to call the attention of the Board of Trustees to the proceedings of their Board held on August 2nd, 1854, and another meeting held on 3rd October of the same year, also to the proceedings at a meeting of the Board held 20th June, 1855. At this last named meeting the powers to be exercised by the Medical Faculty are defined, and the sources whence they are to derive their emoluments distinctly stated in the following words, viz :—

"That no portion of the funds of the University be devoted to the support of the Medical Faculty, but the Professors shall derive their emoluments from their fees, and such other sources as may by the liberality of the Government or of individuals be specially devoted to that purpose."

The Medical Faculty also begs leave to assure the Board of Trustees that if one of its members made any arrangements with the Board relative to the partitioning of the Government grant, and allotting it to special purposes, such a proposition was never submitted to the Medical Faculty, and consequently could never have received its sanction.

The members of the Medical Faculty further desire to assure the Trustees, that whilst in all matters in which the Senate has jurisdiction, the Medical Professors have a vote, yet they have always abstained from exercising that prerogative, and have not even obtruded their opinions at any time on matters relating to the Faculties of Theology and Arts. However, when the Senate is viewed as a whole, the members of the Medical Faculty feel that their duties are as clearly defined and as conscientiously discharged as those of the other Faculties of which the Senate is composed, whilst, it must be conceded, their responsibilities are far greater ; consequently the Medical Faculty is as jealous of the interests, and would desire to protect the honor of the Senate as unsullied, as any of the other Faculties, and would therefore submit that it would be most prejudicial to the interests of the University, and unjust to the Medical Students, to restrict the meetings of the Senate to the time specified in the 69th Clause of the Statutes, as past experience has proven that it is impossible, during the College Session, to make provisions for the many contingencies that always arise during the recess.

In reference to the 27th Clause of the Statutes, the Medical Faculty feels that a great insult is offered to the understanding and judgment of the entire Senate, although they feel at the same time assured that it has been done unwittingly. However, there it stands recorded that

13

tho
man
Coll
with
und

is an
by t

chare
subm
the N
harm

point
Proc

Dra. 1
tho Tr
Facult

the Bo

prosen
sos, an
Board

the members of the Senate, some of whom have been long connected with Queen's College, and many of whom have made sacrifices to advance its best interests, and to whom, as a whole, the College is mainly indebted for its success, are now told that they are no longer to be entrusted with the powers conferred upon them by the Charter, but that henceforth, in judgment and understanding, one member is to outweigh the twelve others of whom the Senate is composed.

The Medical Faculty would therefore submit, that the Senate should meet whenever there is any legitimate business to transact, and that all their proceedings should be valid when signed by the Chairman for the time being, whoever he may be

The Medical Faculty looks on the 15th Clause as very objectionable, as it would lower the character and status of the Senate in the eyes of the Students, and they would respectfully submit that the Board of Trustees would not be a competent Court to review the decisions of the Medical Faculty, and consequently the results in such cases would not tend to promote the harmony that should subsist between the Trustees and the various Faculties.

The Medical Faculty refrains from offering any farther opinion on the other objectionable points of the Statutes, as they have already concurred in what has been put on record in the Proceedings of the Senate.

It was unanimously agreed, on motion of Dr. Litchfield, seconded by Dr. Lavell, that Drs. Dickson, Yates, and Fowler be a Committee to confer with any Committee nominated by the Trustees respecting the Statutes, Rules, and Ordinances for the government of the Medical Faculty of Queen's College.

The above extract was duly communicated by the Dean of the Faculty to the Secretary of the Board of Trustees, but no reply has been received.

In consequence of which, at a meeting of the Medical Faculty, held 25th August, 1863—present, Dr. Dickson, Dean of the Faculty, in the Chair; Professors Litchfield, Fowler, Lawson, and O. Yates—it was resolved, That the Faculty desires to bring under the notice of the Board of Trustees the Resolutions passed by the Faculty on 21st March, 1863, requesting a conference on the subject of the Statutes, and that said Resolutions be herewith printed for the consideration of the Board.

QUEEN'S COLLEGE, KINGSTON, *September*, 1863.

X

MEETING OF PROFESSORS.

SENATE ROOM, QUEEN'S COLLEGE, KINGSTON, *3rd September*, 1863.

A meeting of the resident Professors of Queen's College was held in the Senate Room on 3rd September, 1863. Present, Professors WILLIAMSON, DICKSON, WEIR, FOWLER, LAWSON, KENNEDY and MURRAY. The following Professors, although not present at the meeting, have seen the following resolutions, and concurred in them, viz.: Professors O. YATES, LAVELL, LITCHFIELD and H. YATES.

com
tion
Stat
Sena
held
stam
the (

appo
Com
under
mana
eratio
tract
Colle;
subni
Again
Regul
Senat
Truste
exami
Mr. D
1862,
likewi:
that fi
Macu
Paton
of the
thems
not al
promo
suffici
was ag
Comm
Truste
genera
Januai
agreen
draft o
and Mi
Truste
Board.
the not
loft var
meeting
and the
in the :

53

It was unanimously Resolved to bring again under the notice of the Board of Trustees two communications that were made to the Board by the Senate in March, 1863, upon which no action has been taken by the Board. The communications referred to related to the Code of Statutes which was drawn up by Dr. LEITCH, without consultation or communication with the Senate or any of his colleagues, and which was approved of at a meeting of the Board of Trustees held on 26th January, 1863, at which ten members were present. In order to a proper understanding of the subject, it is necessary to recite some of the facts connected with the passing of the Code of Statutes and Ordinances.

A Committee of Trustees, consisting of Rev. Drs. LEITCH and MACHAR and Mr. PATON, was appointed on 12th December, 1861, to draft Statutes. The Session having passed, while this Committee had made no report, the Senate, at a meeting held on the 4th August, 1862, "had under consideration the desirability of the adoption by the Trustees of by-laws for the internal management of the affairs of the University, and agreed to bring the matter under their consideration." Again, at a meeting of the Senate held on the 13th August, 1862, *inter alia*, "an extract from proceedings of a meeting of the Board of Trustees of the University of Queen's College, held 11th August, 1862, was read, in which the Senate are requested to prepare and submit for the approval of the Trustees a Code of Laws for the government of the College." Again, at a meeting of the Senate held on the 6th September, 1862, the draft of By-Laws and Regulations for the government of the College was revised and corrected, and afterwards the Senate unanimously agreed to instruct the Secretary to transmit a copy thereof to the Board of Trustees. This draft was laid before the Trustees on 8th September, 1862, and referred "for examination and report" to a Committee of their number—Rev. Drs. LEITCH and WILLIAMSON, Mr. DRUMMOND, and Mr. PATON. After the return of Dr. LEITCH from Scotland in November, 1862, the Committee met. Two members of this Committee—Dr. LEITCH and Mr. PATON—had likewise been members of the first appointed Committee of 11th December, 1861 ; and although that first appointed Committee had never met for the purposes of their appointment, and Dr. MACHAR, one of its most important members, was now on his deathbed, they (Dr. LEITCH and Mr. PATON) refused to obey the instructions of the Board "to examine and report" upon the draft of the Statutes carefully drawn up by the Senate at the request of the Trustees, and insisted on themselves preparing a draft of laws, as if the original Committee were still complete, and had not already been virtually discharged by a subsequent appointment of the Board. In order to promote harmonious action, and prevent any unpleasantness, and in the full expectation that sufficient time would be given for the examination and consideration of both by the Board, it was agreed in Committee that two drafts of Statutes—one by the remaining two members of the Committee above referred to, and that drawn up by the Senate—should be submitted to the Trustees, with the recommendation that both should be printed, in order that the Board at its general meeting might select from either as it saw fit. This was reported to the Trustees on 21st January, 1863. But in consequence of certain members of that Committee not fulfilling the agreement and recommendation of their own report, the local Board agreed to print only the draft of Statutes prepared, without the slightest communication with the Senate, by Dr. LEITCH and Mr. PATON, while the one which had been drawn up by the Senate at the request of the Trustees themselves, and concurred in by the several Faculties, was never even read before the Board. This meeting of the local Board was held on Wednesday, the 21st January, 1863, and the notices calling the general meeting for the following Monday, 26th January, could not have left earlier than Thursday, so that it was impossible for the more distant Trustees to be at the meeting, to say nothing of the inconvenience of the day—Monday. Only some of the Trustees, and those not the more distant, were telegraphed to. In short, all the Trustees were not notified in the same manner of the general meeting ; the printed draft was not sent down to them that

the,
ed i
har
opi
diti
viev
Seu

Seu
Univ
Chu
Trus

Com
consi
to be
an h
forw
ccom
was d
" Sou

the T.

they might calmly by themselves consider the proposed Statutes, the proofs having been received from the printer only on the very afternoon of the day of meeting, at which 109 Statutes were hurriedly, and almost without consideration, passed. As several of these Statutes are, in our opinion, injurious to the interests of the College, contrary to the Royal Charter, and to the conditions, expressed or implied, under which we accepted office, we trust you will impartially review the whole circumstances, and take into your favourable consideration the statements of the Senate herewith appended.

We beg leave also to remark that besides the Statutes referred to in the statements of the Senate, there are several others, as for example, that relating to change of the name of the University, and § 107, which we believe to be contrary to the last clauses of §§ 2 and 19 of the Charter, and objectionable in themselves, and to which we beg leave to draw the attention of the Trustees.

After the Statutes were passed, the Senate met on 1st February, 1863, and appointed a Committee, consisting of Rev. Drs. LEITCH and WILLIAMSON, Dr. DICKSON and Dr. LAWSON, to consider the Statutes, and draw up a statement for submission to the Trustees, said statement to be brought before the Senate on 24th February, 1863. Principal LEITCH, however, called, at an hour's notice, a meeting of "Senatus," to be held early on that very day, at which was brought forward a motion by Prof. MURRAY, approving generally of the Statutes, which motion was seconded by Prof. MOWAT, and although no one except the mover and seconder voted for it, it was declared carried by the Principal, who, on the same afternoon, stated to the Senate that the "Senatus" had *unanimously* approved of the Statutes.

The Extracts from Minutes of the Senate, herewith printed, and to which the attention of the Trustees is respectfully requested, will explain the further action of the Senate.

Extract Minutes of the Proceedings of the Senate of Queen's College, Kingston, C. W.

QUEEN'S COLLEGE, *20th February*, 1863.

This day the College Senate met, and was constituted ; the Very Rev. Principal in the chair. Sederunt, Professors MOWAT, WILLIAMSON, WEIR, LAWSON, MURRAY, DICKSON, H. YATES, LAVELL, and KENNEDY.

Inter alia.

It was agreed to request Doctors LEITCH, WILLIAMSON, DICKSON and LAWSON, to examine the Statutes, and to prepare a statement embodying any necessary inquiries or suggestions, with a view to submission to the Board of Trustees, said statement to be laid before the Senate at next meeting.

Extracted from the Minutes of the Senate of Queen's College by

(Signed,)   JOHN C. MURRAY,
Secretary to the Senate.

Inter A

I
agroo
nanco
tho F
oxpor
adapt
requi
prouc

P
and W
rolatir

E

Kinos

T
chair.
O. Y

Inter a

T

55

QUEEN'S COLLEGE, 24th *February*, 1863.

Which day the Senatus met, and was duly constituted by the Principal. Sederunt, The Very Reverend Principal LEITCH, Professors WILLIAMSON, MOWAT, LAWSON, MURRAY and WEIR.

Inter Alia.

It was moved by Professor MURRAY, and seconded by Professor MOWAT, that "The Senatus agree to record their satisfaction with the provisions of the Code of Statutes, Rules and Ordinances recently framed and enacted by the Board of Trustees as far as the said Code relates to the Faculties of Arts and Theology. Though some modifications will probably be suggested by experience, they regard the Code, as far as it affects the said two Faculties, as on the whole adapted to the Constitution of the University, and they therefore hope that, in obedience to its requirements, they may be able more efficiently to perform their duties as Professors, and to promote the general welfare of the Institution."

Professors MURRAY and MOWAT voted for the above motion. Professors WILLIAMSON, LAWSON and WEIR declined voting. The Secretary was instructed to transmit an extract of the minute relating to this matter to the Trustee Board.

Extracted from the Minutes of Senatus by

(Signed,)   GEORGE WEIR,

Secretary.

KINGSTON. *8th September*, 1863. .

———

QUEEN'S COLLEGE, 24th *February*, 1863.

This day the College Senate met, and was constituted ; the Very Rev. Principal in the chair. Sederunt, Professors MOWAT, WILLIAMSON, WEIR, LAWSON, MURRAY, DICKSON, H. YATES, O. YATES, FOWLER, LAVELL, and KENNEDY.

Inter alia.

The following Report of the Committee appointed to examine the Statutes was received :—

SENATE ROOM, QUEEN'S COLLEGE, 21st *February*, 1863.

The Committee appointed by the Senate met this day, present, The Very Rev. Principal LEITCH, Professors WILLIAMSON, DICKSON, and LAWSON, and in accordance with their instructions drafted the following statement for submission to the Board of Trustees :—

To THE HONORABLE THE BOARD OF TRUSTEES OF QUEEN'S COLLEGE, KINGSTON :

The members of the Senate of Queen's College, feeling deeply the importance of maintaining unimpaired that harmony of feeling and of action which has hitherto uniformly existed between the Board of Trustees and the Senate, beg respectfully to submit to your Honorable Board the

14

following statement, with the request that you will be pleased to take the same into your consideration as embodying the views of the Senate relative to certain Statutes recently passed by your Board. In reference to

Statute 10. The Senate is of opinion that the penalties enumerated in the 15th clause of the Charter, namely, admonition, reproof, suspension, or removal of the Principal and Professors, can only be inflicted after a complaint being first made and proven with reference to impropriety of conduct, and that therefore no Professor now holds his tenure of office merely during the pleasure of the Board of Trustees.

St. 15. The Senate is of opinion that the Board of Trustees is not constituted by the Charter a Court of Review over the Senate in decisions upon the qualifications of candidates for degrees or conferring of the same.

St. 18. The Senate would respectfully direct attention to this Statute as liable to misconstruction in its present form.

St. 20. The Senate is of opinion that the annual Calendar should be prepared by the Principal, after communication with the various Faculty Boards, and should be submitted to the Senate preparatory to its being laid before the annual meeting of Trustees for approval.

St. 26. The Senate is of opinion that diplomas should be signed not only by the Principal, but also by at least four Professors, in terms of the 24th clause of the Charter. This 26th Statute, and also Statute 25, 62-68, relate to degrees, the regulation of which devolves by the Charter upon the Senate, and should therefore be embodied in the By-laws of the Senate rather than in the general Statutes of the University.

St. 27. The Senate is of opinion that the proceedings of any meeting of Senate legally constituted should be valid when signed by the Chairman of said meeting.

St. 35. The Senate is of opinion that the Professors now in office were appointed to perform the duties belonging to their respective Chairs, and came under no obligation to perform any other. If they undertake additional duties, it is entirely at their own option.

St. 53. Exemption from attendance on prayers being a matter of College discipline, belongs properly to the College Senate.

St. 59. The College Senate is of opinion that, as no exception is made in the Charter, all persons whatever resident in the College are placed under the Academical superintendence and discipline of the Senate.

St. 60. This Statute, requiring inquiry, proof, and record of the action of the Senate in reviewing the conduct of the Students, should be a By-Law of the Senate to regulate cases of discipline.

St. 69. The Senate is of opinion that there can be no limitation as to the time at which necessary meetings of the Senate shall be held, and that it would be most injurious to the in-

Re
already
Faculty
tenth S
ting to
of Tru

Th
Sederu

in'er atia

It
mittee
24th F
with a
the su

O
for it

57

terests of the College that the time should be limited to the College Session; and that if any member, when a meeting is called, is absent in another part of the Province, he can be notified by circular, when all will be placed on the same footing in this respect.

Resolved, That the first clause of the Report relative to Statute X. be adopted.

Resolved further,* That as the Principal has explained to the meeting that the Senatus has already expressed an opinion on the Statutes, and that he intends to bring them before the other Faculty Boards, all that portion of the Committee's Report after the paragraph relating to the tenth Statute be simply recorded in the Minutes of the Senate: further, that that portion relating to the tenth Statute, along with the preamble, be transmitted to the Secretary of the Board of Trustees.

QUEEN'S COLLEGE, 10th *April*, 1863.

This day the College Senate met, and was constituted; the Very Rev. Principal in the chair. Sederunt, Professors WILLIAMSON, WEIR, MOWAT, LAWSON, MURRAY, DICKSON, LAVELL and KENNEDY.

Inter alia.

It was moved by Dr. WILLIAMSON, seconded by Dr. LAWSON, That the Report of the Committee on the Statutes, received by the Senate, and recorded in the Minutes of the Senate of the 24th February last, be hereby adopted, and ordered to be transmitted to the Board of Trustees, with a respectful request that the Trustees will take into consideration, at their first full meeting, the suggestions and statements contained in said Report.

On the motion being put, Professors WILLIAMSON, WEIR, LAWSON, DICKSON and KENNEDY voted for it; Professor MURRAY against it; Professors MOWAT and LAVELL declining to vote.

Extracted from the Minutes of the Senate of Queen's College by

(Signed,)   JOHN C. MURRAY,
Secretary to the Senate

XI.

Extract from the proceedings at an adjourned meeting of the Board of Trustees of the University of Queen's College, held on the 10th day of February, 1864.

Resolved, That from the facts which have come to the knowledge of the Trustees, and the present alarming state of the College, the Trustees deem it necessary, in the interest of the College, to remove Professor WEIR from the Offices of Professor of Classics and Secretary to the Senatus, and in the exercise of their power to remove at discretion, they hereby do remove him

---
* On the motion of Professor LAWSON, seconded by Professor MURRAY, and unanimously agreed to.

from these offices accordingly forthwith, and that the Treasurer do pay to him his salary in full to the end of the present Session, and for six months thereafter, in advance, in lieu of notice, and that the Secretary be instructed to communicate this resolution to Mr. WEIR.

Extracted from the Minutes of proceedings of

W. IRELAND,
Secretary to Board of Trustees.

EXHIBITS.

Produced at the Examination of Witnesses on the 26th, 27th and 28th September, 1864.

"A."

Referred to in the evidence of George Malloch.

Queen's College, Kingston, 2nd February, 1864.

DEAR SIR,—An adjourned meeting of the Trustees of Queen's College is appointed to be held on Wednesday the 3rd instant. On that day the meeting will be further adjourned till Tuesday, the 9th of February, instant, at seven o'clock in the evening, in order that a communication received from Principal Leitch, which has been addressed to me by that officer, "intimating "that circumstances have arisen in the College which urgently demand the immediate action of "the Board of Trustees," may be considered, and that such action may be taken by the Board as the circumstances to be laid before the Board may be found to require.

I have, therefore, to request your punctual attendance on that day.
I have the honor to be,
Your obedient servant,
JOHN HAMILTON,
Chairman.

"B."

Referred to in the evidence of George Malloch.

Brockville, 3rd February, 1864.

DEAR SIR,—Late last evening I received your notice of yesterday's date, informing me that "an adjourned meeting of the Trustees of Queen's College is appointed to be held on Wednesday, the 3rd instant, on that day the meeting will be further adjourned till Tuesday, the 9th day of February, instant, at 7 o'clock in the evening, &c."

I cannot see how there can be a regular adjourned meeting for this day, no hour stated, nor has there been a meeting called according to the 29th, 30th and 31st sections of the Charter, the meeting of the first October last, when I was present, having broken up without adjournment.

f at
ters for
writing
incurred
disappoi

To Hos.
      C.

      R

Sin,
notice th
held in t
noon.
  Desi
will be n
Estate l
January,
10th Fel
fessor, o
meeting
tees may
will be e
ther not
the Syn
of those

I attended a meeting last year, according to notice, for the consideration of important matters for the well-being of the College, and because the meeting was not required to be called in writing according to the 107th Statute, I had to return without considering the business, having incurred unnecessary expense. I have no intention at present of exposing myself to such another disappointment.

I have the honour to be,
Your obedient servant,
(Signed,)   GEO. MALLOCH.

To Hon. JOHN HAMILTON,
    Chairman Board of Trustees,
        Queen's College, Kingston.

" C."

Referred to in the evidence of Wm. Ireland.

Queen's College at Kingston, 27th April, 1864.

Sir,—In pursuance of the request, a copy of which is hereunto annexed, I hereby give you notice that a General Meeting of the Board of Trustees of Queen's College, at Kingston, will be held in the College Senate Chamber on Tuesday, the 31st May next, at four o'clock in the afternoon.

Besides the transaction of all business usually transacted at a General Meeting, resolutions will be moved for filling up all vacant Chairs and Offices in the College; for the disposal of Real Estate belonging to the College; and also for the confirmation of the meetings of the 26th January, 1863, at which certain Statutes, Rules, and Ordinances, were passed, and of the 9th and 10th February, 1864, at which the Reverend George Weir was removed from the office of Professor, or that such other action may be taken in reference to the matters dealt with at the said meetings of the 26th January, 1863, and 9th and 10th February, 1864, as to the Board of Trustees may seem meet. I hereby also notify you that the report of the committee on the Statutes will be considered and such action taken thereon as the Board may deem necessary. And I further notify you that on the 1st day of June next being the first day of the ensuing meeting of the Synod, the Lay Trustees will meet for the purpose of appointing new Trustees in the place of those who retire in rotation pursuant to the Charter.

I am, Sir,
Your obedient Servant,
JNO HAMILTON,
Chairman,

18th April, 1864.

The Hon JOHN HAMILTON,
    Chairman of the Board of Trustees, Queen's College, Kingston:

Sir,—The technical regularity of the adjourned Meetings of the Board of Trustees of Queen's College at Kingston having been called in question, though they have been adjourned agreeably to the practice of the Board ever since the College was established, and inasmuch as

15

THE

hope
satis

held

it is desirable that no pretence of this sort should thwart or render questionable what is or may be considered for the interests of the College, we hereby request you to summon a General Meeting of the Board of Trustees to be held at Kingston on Tuesday, the 31st day of May next, in the manner directed by the Charter.

Your obedient servants,

(Signed,) HUGH URQUHART,
(Signed,) DUNCAN MORRISON, } *Trustees.*
(Signed,) ALEXANDER SPENCE,

—

" D."

Referred to in the evidence of Wm. Ireland.

University of Queen's College, Kingston, 12th Nov., 1859.

The Reverend Professor WEIR,
    Queen's College,

Rev. and Dear Sir,—I have much pleasure in handing you the written extract, by which, I hope, everything which might mar the harmony and pleasant feeling in our College has been satisfactorily adjusted.

Yours, very truly,

(Signed,) JOHN PATON,
        Secretary.

———

" E."

See ante No. 8 of documents produced by Plaintiff under order for production.

— ... —

" F."

Queen's College, Kingston, 2nd February, 1861.

Dear Sir,—An adjourned meeting of the Trustees of Queen's College is appointed to be held on Wednesday the 3rd instant. On that day the meeting will be further adjourned till Tuesday, the 9th of February, instant, at 7 o'clock in the evening, in order that a communication from Principal Leitch, which has been addressed to me by that officer, intimating that circumstances have arisen in the College which urgently demand the immediate action of the Board of Trustees, may be considered, and that such action may be taken by the Board as the circumstances to be laid before the Board may be found to require.

I have therefore to request your punctual attendance on that day.

I have the honour to be,
    Your obedient servant,
(Signed,) JOHN HAMILTON,
        Chairman.

S...
tee of
7 o'clo...

Business...
late...
Se...

M...

I s...
scheme...
wrote t...
you wo...
Synod l...
jority, ...
bly, it i...
in a few...

It i...
chief q...
be sati...
that we...
secure...
life app...
church...
thing t...
an imp...
would...
I were...
the offi...

64

"G."

Referred to in the evidence of Wm. Ireland.

University of Queen's College, Kingston, 5th February, 1864.

Sir,— Your attendance is respectfully requested at a general adjourned meeting of the Trustees of Queen's College, to be held in the Senate Chamber on Tuesday next, the 9th instant, at 7 o'clock, P. M.

(Signed.) W. IRELAND,
Secretary to the Board of Trustees.

Business.
Inter alia
New circular of 2nd instant.

"H."

Referred to in the evidence of Wm. Ireland.

Monimail Manse, Lady Bank, 16th July, 1861.

My Dear Sir,— I have received your very welcome letter.

* * * * *

I suppose you have by this time received a letter (a similar one was sent to Mr. Morris) with scheme for the consideration of Trustees in the event of the union taking place. I think I also wrote to Dr. Machar on the subject. The object of the letter was simply to say that I hoped you would not make any claim of mine a bar to the union of Colleges. You answered that the Synod has delayed the Union by a majority of 9. Taking into account the smallness of the majority, and that the Synod had not probably by that time received the deliverance of the assembly, it is not improbable that by another year the majority may lie in the other way, at least that in a few years the growth of feeling may be so great as to necessitate a union.

It is right to look this union in the face and consider how it will affect the College. The chief question is, is it not of advantage that the College should be free to elect a head that would be satisfactory to the majority of the uniting bodies. Would it be wise to impose any fetters that would prevent an amalgamation of Colleges. Then as to my position it would not be a secure one. Were things to remain as at present, I would consider my situation as good as a life appointment, but when the Trustees change and the majority have no sympathy with old church principles, as will partly be the case when the union is effected, it will be a very natural thing that another should be put in my place. According to the Charter I might be removed for an impropriety, proved to the satisfaction of the Trustees, and if there was any party bias, as would likely be the case in the event of the union, some impropriety could readily be found. If I were freely elected after the union by a Board representing all parties, then I would consider the office secure enough.

The only plan that occurs to me of securing the office in the event of a union is the guaranteeing of a life salary, which, I think, the Charter admits of. The following does not imply any personal responsibility and is not at the expense of the other Professors.

the
plea
sala

sala
not b

Chap

depri
tiring

It do
my cl
bar to
I cam
the m
secur
the ii
lege,
incon
not g
will n
proba
ests o

"That the Queen's College engage to pay Dr. Leitch, as Principal of the College, a salary of £600 under the following conditions.

"1st. That if the funds of the College suffer any abatement, so as to lead to a diminution of the salaries of the other existing chairs in Arts and Theology, Dr. Leitch's salary may at the pleasure of the Trustees be reduced to an extent not exceeding the proportion in which the salaries of these chairs taken as a whole are reduced.

"2nd. That in like manner should the funds of the College be augmented, and the other salaries in Arts and Theology be increased, Dr. Leitch's salary shall be increased in a proportion not less than the other salaries in Arts and Theology are as a whole increased.

"3rd. That in the event of Dr. Leitch being deprived of the status of a minister of the Church of Scotland, all payment to him by the College shall cease.

"4th. That if Dr. Leitch be removed from the office of Principal on any other ground than deprivation of his status as a minister of the Church of Scotland, the College shall pay him a retiring allowance of not less than two-thirds of his salary at the time of removal."

The principle of the above is the sharing of the fortunes of the College whether good or bad. It does not restrict the power of removal at any time. In the event of a union it might secure my claim to continuance in the office, but then you must equally keep in view that it might be a bar to amalgamation; while you secure my position you may injure the interests of the College. I cannot urge upon you a security which may interfere with the free election of a Principal of the united churches, and at the same time you would not expect me to accept a position so insecure. You ought to balance these considerations, and do not hesitate to sacrifice my claims if the interests of the College require this. This is evidently the crisis of the history of the College, and on the wisdom of the steps now taken must depend its future prosperity. The present inconvenience by delaying to make a permanent appointment is, no doubt, great, but may you not gain by it future permanent advantages. Although the time of union is uncertain, still all will allow that it is probable within a short period, and it is right to make provision for that probability. Would it, therefore, be prudent to elect a permanent Principal now when the interests of the College may soon require a new appointment. The amalgamation of Colleges for example may require that you should elect the Principal of the Free College. I should wish the Trustees gravely to consider this matter. The two chief points are, would it not better delay a permanent appointment, and in the meantime to appoint a Vice-Principal, and if this be injurious to the interests of the College, would such a security as I have above suggested be given. I have to repeat that in this consideration the Trustees are to look simply to the interests of the College, without any regard to any claims of mine upon the office. I need not say how much in every way the situation is suited to my tastes. I can honestly say that I never spent a half year of my life more pleasantly and profitably to myself, and that I do not expect ever to occupy a situation productive of greater happiness; still no selfish enjoyment would lead me to insist on retaining an office which the interests of the College may require to be assigned to another.

I am glad to learn that the governors have so liberally agreed to erect an operating theatre. I am sure I have no reason to complain of the readiness of the Kingston people to aid in my good work. The College will prosper just in proportion as we form links of connection between the College and the Town, such as the Observatory, Botanic Society, Hospital.

I
of To

I
under
matte
recogn
Act h

I
in my

V
the M
negoti

63

I am glad that our agitation is likely to bear some fruit already. A share of the endowment of Toronto University would put Queen's on a natural basis, and greatly increase its efficiency.

I am busy at present corresponding with the various Universities and Medical Schools in order to define our relation to them. There has been a complete revolution lately in University matters, so that it is difficult to ascertain how things actually stand. I hope, however, to get a recognition of the Courses at Queen's College both in Arts and Medicine. The late Medical Act however bears injuriously against Colonial degrees.

I have lately explained my position to my Presbytery, and the Presbytery cordially acquiesce in my decision.

Would you have the goodness to ask Professor Lawson to send me half a dozen copies of the Medical programme, and the programme for degrees in Arts, as I require to use them in negotiating with the Medical bodies.

I remain,
Yours very truly,

(Signed.)   WILLIAM LEITCH.

" I."

Referred to in the evidence of Wm. Ireland.
(Extract)

Montreal, 3rd August, 1861.

DEAR PATON,

The fact is I regard the Dr.'s difficulties as myths. The appointment is now a permanent one, and there is little likelihood of any culpa so grave as to require his removal. The security is only sought in event of removal.

Yours truly,

(Signed.)   A. MORRIS.

" K."

Referred to in the evidence of Wm. Ireland.

Hamilton, 6th August, 1861.

MY DEAR SIR,—Will you be good enough to state to the Board of Trustees of Queen's College, at the meeting on Thursday next, my opinion that the Board should agree to the stipulations contained in Dr. Leitch's letter. As he appears from the tenor of his letter to be under a misapprehension as to the permanency of his appointment, I think that while we assent to his

16

ately
and v

I
seare!

t
me, a
the la

terms without any restriction, he should be informed that the appointment was a permanent one, and that he has acquired a position and status of which he cannot be deprived without sufficient cause, that it is in fact a life appointment.   *   *   *

I am,
Dear sir,
Yours very truly,
(Signed),   A. LO IR.

WM. IRELAND, ESQ.
   Secretary of Board of Trustees
   of Queen's College.

" L."

Referred to in the evidence of William Ireland.

DEAR SIR,—I enclose you two testimonials of Professor Weir, the only ones I can immediately lay my hands upon, but one of them, I mean Mr. Menzies's letter, that which decided me, and which as reported by me, decided the Trustees, who referred the whole to Mr. Menzies.

If you would ascertain from Mr. Weir what other testimonials I had from him I would make search for them.

I do not see why Dr. McGill's remarks should make you resign, if there was blame, it was with me, and I counsel you to pay no attention to anything that may have been said, but let me bear the burden.

Yours truly,
JOHN COOK.

Quebec, 12th June.

" M."

Referred to in the evidence of William Ireland.

DEAR SIR,— I have much pleasure in informing you that I have received a letter from Professor Menzies, of Edinburgh, informing me that Mr. Weir has accepted the Classical Professorship of Queen's College, and will be in the field in October. Gobbes, as you are aware, had been appointed Master of the Grammar School, Aberdeen. Weir will, I am persuaded, be an acquisition.

I am anxious to hear what has been done about the house of the Archdeacon, and whether any negotiation has been entered into with the Government. The absence of Mr. Morris from Quebec, has prevented me from doing anything, I think he should be sounded, but if it is wished, I will see Mr. Hincks.

I have not yet answered Mr. Morris' communication to myself; but this I think of less consequence, as no Principal can be found for this Session, and George will well perform th duties. Besides, the result of the negotiation with the Government should be ascertained, for the security of the Trustees in assuming such liabilities, and for the security of any one who may ultimately be appointed Principal: at least such are my views. I shall count it a favor if you will let me know what is doing.

I am, with much respect,

Dear Sir,

Yours truly,

JOHN COOK.

Quebec, 17th September, 1853.

The Hon. J. Hamilton, &c., &c.

You will be sorry to hear of Mr. Morris's condition.

J. C.

———

" N. "

Referred to in the evidence of William Ireland.

Montreal, 26th September, 1853.

The Hon. John Hamilton,

Chairman Trustees, Queen's College.

DEAR SIR,—The lamented illness of the Hon. William Morris, Chairman of the Sub-Committee appointed at the last meeting of Trustees, to select and recommend for appointment Professors to fill the vacancies in the Staff of the College, devolves on me the necessity of communicating with you on the subject.

The Committee, agreeably to their instructions, wrote to Professor Menzies, of Edinburgh, and through him have been fortunate enough to secure the services, as Classical Professor, of the Rev. Mr. Weir, of Banff, who may be expected in Kingston next month, say October.

The Committee offered the Principalship (the only other vacancy) to the Reverend Dr. Cook, of Quebec, giving him till the 10th September to reply. His answer is to the effect that if you can make any arrangement whereby his salary will be secured to him, he will accept the appointment, and enter heartily into the performance of its duties; but as he has a large family, and is now well situated as regards pecuniary affairs, he would be wanting in his duty to them if he gave up a certainty for an uncertainty. He therefore suggests that as he could not, in any case, join the College this session, the matter be delayed for the present to see if anything can be done with the Government for an increased grant to the College, and he says that this course will not entail any inconvenience, as Mr. George, from his unpreparedness for the Chair of Morals, wished to teach Theology for another session.

on
for

this
Gov

W. In

S
of Qu
I am n
Board
cipal I
the ino

I
duty o
be tra
given
chairn
arisen

I :
within
and th
warnin
ical in
specific

I t
the Se
which
involve
ance.

The Committee feel so anxious to secure the services of Dr. Cook, that they are inclined to act on his suggestion, more especially as they have not at present any other in view so well qualified for the situation.

Will you therefore be pleased to consult with the Trustees in Kingston and let me know if this course meets their approval ; meantime I will endeavour to effect some arrangement with the Government.

I am, Dear Sir,
Yours, faithfully.
HUGH ALLAN.
Secretary Committee of Trustees.

" O. "

Referred to in the evidence of William Ireland.

TO BE COMMUNICATED.

W. IRELAND. Esq.
Secretary to the Board of Trustees of Queen's College.

Sir,--I have received your circular informing me than an adjourned meeting of the Trustees of Queen's College is to take place on Thursday, the 9th inst., at 7 o'clock in the evening, and I am referred by you to another circular, which I have also received from the Chairman of the Board, stating that such meeting is for the purpose of considering a communication from Principal Leitch, intimating that circumstances have arisen in the College which urgently demand the immediate action of the Board of Trustees.

I beg to state to the Board, through you, that by the 41st Statute of the University it is the duty of the Secretary when sending written notices of the meetings, to specify the business to be transacted ; and I consider it singular that in this case such specifying of the business as is given is by the chairman, and not by the regular officer. In point of fact, however, what the chairman states is quite indefinite : " We are to meet to consider circumstances which have arisen in the College ;" but there is no inkling given of what those circumstances were.

I suppose it possible that the adjournment may be conceived to bring the proposed meeting within the letter of the law. But, in reality, it is a special meeting, and for a special purpose, and the chairman's letter renders it plain that so it was felt to be ; and that to hold it without warning, even though it might be legal, would not be fair or just to the Trustees at a distance ; and in their view it is, I hold, specially necessary that the Secretary's notice should have specified the business to be transacted.

I think no one will dispute the reasonableness of the duty imposed by the Statute 41st on the Secretary, who considers the expense to the College and the trouble to distant Trustees, which attendance on the meetings of the Board involves. In my case and Mr. Thompson's it involves now travelling eight hundred miles in midwinter. I can readily conceive that circumstances might arise in the College which urgently demand the immediate action of the Board,

given
of su
of co
ing,
night
two,
acco
are to
a jou

which yet, if plainly stated, the Trustees at a distance would be perfectly willing to trust to the management of the Trustees in Kingston and the neighbourhood of Kingston. But I can also conceive circumstances of the like kind, in regard of which it would be better and safer for all concerned that the Trustees at a distance should be present at the meeting, and take part in the deliberations of the Board. I hold it a just ground of complaint, that no opportunity has been given of enabling us to judge whether the circumstances to be considered, are, or are not, of such a nature as to require special attendance. I do further think, that there is just ground of complaint in that Tuesday, rather than Wednesday, has been appointed as the day of meeting. It is just possible that after p___ming my Sunday duties, I could by travelling day and night at this inclement season, and if nothing occurred to delay the railway train an hour or two, reach King___on in time for the proposed meeting. Heretofore it has been usual to take into account the convenience of Trustees at a distance, and unless the unknown circumstances which are to be considered are very urgent, indeed I think another day might have been given for so long a journey ___ ___ of us have to take when we attend the meetings of the Board.

One ___ ___ ___ of Statute 41, and the fact that though nominally an adjourned, it is really a special me___ ___, the business to be transacted at which is not specified in the Secretary's notice, I protest against the meeting as altogether irregular and illegal.

I am, Sir,

Your obedient servant,

JOHN COOK.

Quebec, 8th Feb., 1861.

" P. "

Referred to in the evidence of Charles Peters.

At Banff, the sixth day of August, one thousand eight hundred and fifty years. In a meeting of the Managers. Present—Messrs. Hosswick, Balfour and Gordon.

Mr. Gordon stated, That in consequence of last Minute, he, Mr. Hosswick, and the Clerk, have gone to Banff last Saturday, and have seen Mr. George Weir and the classes taught by him, and had every reason to be satisfied with the manner in which he performed his duties: and being satisfied on this point, had broken the subject to Mr. Weir coming to Banff to him when he had requested a few days for consideration, and promised to be here this day, and that he understood that Mr. Weir was now in attendance ; and Mr. Weir having been called in, and a long consultation having ensued between him and the Managers, in the course of which he expressed his inclination to accept of the appointment of Rector, if the terms could be made agreeable to him ; and a farther conversation having ensued there anent, it was resolved that Mr. Weir should be, and he is hereby appointed Rector of the Academy and Grammar School, and teacher of the classical, mathematical and writing departments thereof, at the yearly salary of sixty pounds sterling, his engagement to commence on the ninth day of September next, and to be *ad vitam aut culpam*, it being understood that his share of the fees from Bursar is to be the subject of arrangement between the Patron of the Bursars, and himself, and the teacher of the English departments ; and that the Managers will meet with him and the English teacher before said date, to revise the scale of fees for the various branches to be taught, the hour of attendance, and other particulars necessary to be settled before the opening of the classes on the

17

c
1
Univ
or by
he re

expiring of the present vacation ; and it being also understood that this appointment shall be subject to such reasonable alterations on details, fees, or internal management as the Manager or the Magistrates and Council may find it necessary to make from time to time ; and that in the event of Mr. Weir wishing to leave, he shall give six months' premonition before doing so ; whereupon, Mr. Weir is declared and hereby declares his acceptance, and the Managers, on the meeting of the School, will install him accordingly.

(Signed,)
GEORGE WEIR,
HENRY BALFOUR,
WILLIAM BOSSWICK,
W. R. GORDON.

Extracted by George Forbes, Town Clerk.

"Q"

Referred to in the evidence of John Cook.

Extract from Statutes of McGill College.

Chapter V.

Of the appointment and duties of Officers, Faculties, High School Department, &c.

1. the Principal, Vice-Principal, Deans of Faculty, Professors, and all other officers of the University (except the Demonstrator of Anatomy who may be appointed by the Medical Faculty or by the Professor of Anatomy, if the Governors so allow or order, and in such case shall be removable at the pleasure either of the party so appointing him or of the Governor) shall be appointed and shall hold office for and during the pleasure of the Governor, and no longer, and they shall receive such salaries and emoluments as may be fixed by the Governors. The several Professors and other officers of the University shall have such titles of Office, and discharge such duties as may from time to time be assigned to them by the Governor.

" R."

See also Exhibit No. 2, referred to in the examination of Plaintiff.

" S. "

Referred to in the evidence of John Cook.

Complaint respecting the conduct of Professor George Weir of Queen's College.

1. That Professor George Weir has been guilty of improper conduct, inasmuch as he did during the month of February or January last cause to be printed by James M. Creighton, of the city of Kingston, an anonymous paper, of which a copy is produced, containing an extract from

the Mi
and ca

2.
copies
and to

3.
in fram
notices

4.
Office,
George
the cha

5.
quest J
submit

Wards

7.

8.
from th
did so a
fessor V
Kingsto

9.
and dis
Februa
ance of

10.
Dr. Gee

11.
Professo
serting

12.
students
with the
to the B

the Minutes of the Board, together with comments upon the same, disrespectful to the Board, and calculated to injure the College.

2. That the said Professor Weir did circulate or cause to be circulated a large number of copies of this printed paper addressed to members of the Board, to Students of the University, and to many other persons in various sections of the Province.

3. That Professor Weir did affix or cause to be affixed a copy of this paper to the blackboard in front of the College during the month of February last, such board being reserved for official notices.

4. That the said Professor Weir did send or cause to be sent through the Kingston Post Office, during the month of February last, a copy of the aforesaid printed paper addressed to Dr. George, "The immoral Professor of Queen's College," such conduct being calculated to injure the character of the University.

5. That Professor Weir did during the month of February last, through a near relative, request John Creighton, of the City of Kingston, to print an anonymous poem, of which a copy is submitted, and afterwards did cause the same to be printed elsewhere.

6. That this poem was sent with Professor Weir's sanction and approval to the Rev. Thomas Wardrope, of the City of Ottawa, The Rev. H. J. Bostwick, and otherwise circulated.

7. That this poem is calculated to injure the Institution, and corrupt the morals of youth.

8. That the said Professor Weir has repeatedly during the past session absented himself from the duties of his class, without permission or proper excuse, and more especially that he did so absent himself on the 24th, 25th, 26th, 27th and 28th days of March last, the said Professor Weir being able on these days to visit and examine the Common Schools of the City of Kingston, and to discharge other equally laborious duties.

9. That the conduct of the said Professor Weir has been improper and subversive of order and discipline in the College, inasmuch as he has repeatedly during the months of January, February and March addressed or spoken to students in his class-room during hours of attendance of College on the case of Dr. George.

10. That he has dissuaded or sanctioned the dissuasion of various students from attending Dr. George's class.

11. That in his class-room, during the months of January, February and March last, the said Professor Weir has read to students many letters and papers strongly commenting and animadverting upon the proceedings of the College authorities.

12. That the conduct of the said Professor Weir has been calculated to injure the morals of students in this University, inasmuch as he did read to several of them certain papers connected with the case of Dr. George, and more especially the affidavit of his sister at one time submitted to the Board.

"T."

Sch... No. 2.

Referred to in the examination of the Plaintiff.

"C."

Referred to in the evidence of John Cook.

Kingston, 7th Nov., 1861.

WILLIAM IRELAND, Esq.,
      Secretary to Board of Trustees of the University of Queen's College.

DEAR SIR,—To prevent any misunderstanding in regard to the investigation which the Trustees have undertaken at Professor George's request, I beg that it will be distinctly understood that in this painful matter I am at present neither accuser or prosecutor. At Professor George's own request, as may be seen by the correspondence between us, I gave him the reason of my refusing to hold any the slightest intercourse with him, viz., that my sister bore a child, of which child she has uniformly and solemnly affirmed the Professor George is the father.

While desirous, as I have already stated, of affording the Trustees every aid in obtaining information and evidence, I wish that my present legal position in the matter should not be misunderstood.

All that I am responsible for is the accuracy of my allegation that the above-mentioned statement was made by another party.

I am, dear Sir,
            Yours truly,
                  GEORGE WEIR.

_____

" V. "

Referred to in the evidence of John C. Murray and Alexander Logie.

Having requested that a general meeting of the Board of Directors should be called, it devolved on me to explain the circumstances which have led me to make the request. By Statute 22, I am required to lay before the Board the conduct of such officers as may require the exercise of discipline. I should gladly have avoided such a painful duty, especially at a time when prostrated by an alarming illness, but the emergency of the case demanded instant action. I felt that if the vital interests of the College were to be protected, prompt and decisive measures must be taken without delay. I would have preferred to wait to the end of the Session, but the evil was so rapidly spreading that irreparable injury might be the consequence of such delay. I shall shortly lay before you the points to which the attention of the Board requires to be directed. It will be with the Board to decide what steps should be taken to remedy the

grave evils which have so seriously damaged the prosperity of the College, and which threaten its very existence.

CASE OF PROFESSOR WEIR.

This is the point that demands the most serious attention of the Trustees. His case has been repeatedly before the Trustees, and he has repeatedly been cautioned as to his conduct, but I regret to say that these cautions have only led to a disregard of the authority of the Board. Each successive caution apparently leading him to treat the authority of the Board with less respect. After three years painful experience of his character, I am led to the unhesitating conclusion that his mental and moral character has now assumed a morbid aspect, and that the malady is rapidly increasing in intensity. This malady consists in an intense love of strife, combined with personal animosity. It assumes the aspect of monomania, by singling out certain individuals or parties as the object of persecution, while to all others he may have the strongest feelings of kindness and goodwill. The necessity of cherishing personal animosity to some one seems to be a necessity of his being, and it is his successive attempts to gratify this feeling that has kept the College in a state of strife for so many years. While I am strongly of opinion that his conduct partakes of the character of insanity, I by no means hold that he is insane, in the sense that he is not personally responsible for his actions. His case is merely that of so many others who have allowed some evil passion to gain the mastery over them.

I shall now state the facts on which the above conclusion is founded. It is about ten years since the strife commenced which has now reached a crisis. With the sad history of the earlier years of strife I am not personally conversant. When I arrived, in the autumn of 1860, in this country, I was not aware that the College had been the scene of such heart-burning and strife for many years previously. And I by no means blame the Trustees for not informing me of this, because I am persuaded that they believed the strife was healed, and, besides, I had afterwards the opportunity of judging for myself, before finally deciding to cast my lot in this country. When I landed in Canada, I heard everywhere of the intestine quarrels which had long existed, and descriptions were given me of the intensity of animosity, which transcended all powers of belief. These accounts appeared to me so highly colored and exaggerated, that I thought them incredible, the hatred and animosity appeared by these accounts to be more than human, and it is only in the light of recent events that I can now credit them. The sad series of strifes commenced with Professor Smith, after a period of cordial friendship. This promising young man he pursued with unrelenting bitterness, till, in the providence of God, he was taken from the evil to come by an early death. The morbid feeling to which I refer seems to have been developed thus early, for not long after his animosity was transferred to Dr. George. This strife raged for a long period, and was carried to such a pitch that the Trustees were compelled to interfere. The expressions of intensity of hatred were so terrible, that the story is more like a romance than a sad reality. The scene before the Trustees when both parties were summoned, is, perhaps, sufficiently remembered by some of the members present to vouch for the accuracy of the statement. A significant warning was given at the time, that such conduct, if persisted in, would be followed by removal. This warning seemed to be effectual for some time, and when I came out in 1860, there appeared to be a calm. I was told on all hands that it was a deceitful calm, that the flames were only smouldering. I was not disposed to believe this, as I found him everything I could wish in the way of personal friendship towards myself. Every expression of kindness was lavished upon me to gain my good will. In this happy state of things, while a temporary peace prevailed, the College made rapid strides. The Law Faculty was established; the Observatory was connected with the College; a Botanical Society was instituted important steps in ad-

18

...aces were taken in the University Question; and the College bade fair to have a successful and brilliant career. It was on the foundation of these bright prospects that I finally resolved to fix my abode in Canada. I little thought there was a spirit slumbering only to awaken with renewed intensity to dash these hopes to the ground.

I went home in the summer of 1861, and on returning to Canada in the fall, the first news I learned on landing was, that the old quarrel with Dr. George had broken out with renewed intensity, and that the occasion of its renewal was the sad story of his sister's shame, which occupied soon after so much of the attention of this Court. It was now that the idea of insanity flashed upon my mind. I did not indeed think it strange that a brother should demand reparation, if he believed the story. He would not be human if he did not feel indignation. The proof of a morbid taint lay in another direction. It consisted chiefly in the want of that dignity and delicacy of feeling which we would expect from a brother towards a fallen sister. He seems to have lost that fine moral sense which would manifest a genuine sorrow for his sister's conduct. This insensibility to his sister's shame was, no doubt, caused by the all-absorbing passion which led him to pursue Dr. George for so many years with unrelenting bitterness. This insensibility was shown in many ways. The letters, with the details of his sister's guilt, were read to all who would listen. Students of tender years, as well as the more advanced, were asked to listen to the most indelicate and licentious details. I often heard him read these letters, and the impression invariably produced in my mind was, that the feeling of satisfaction that he had now crushed his enemy far predominated over the feeling of sadness at his sister's fall, and I have no doubt it was the same impression that caused a shudder of horror, at his conduct, throughout Canada, when the tale of shame was told in connection with the previous quarrel with Dr. George. Another proof of morbid action was, that his animosity to Dr. George became a dominant feeling, characteristic of monomania. It seemed to banish all other ideas, and he loved or hated all others only as they stood related to the object of his anger. All this holds good, whatever view we take, as to the truth of the story. The deep feeling which his conduct excited throughout Canada was altogether irrespective of the truth or falsehood of the charges.

It will be remembered that in the spring of 1862 Professor Weir was again brought up before the Trustees, a complaint being brought against him by one of the Trustees. It arose out of his morbid animosity to Dr. George. Though Dr. George was to retire at the end of the session, yet his presence for a few months so aggravated the morbid feeling of hatred, that he was led to commit the most humiliating acts in order to gratify this feeling. The list of these acts was printed at the time. One of the gravest being a scurrilous poem, clearly traced to him, in which the most libellous charges were brought against Dr. George. The deep feeling caused by this poem was not so much in consequence of the injury done to Dr. George, as the insensibility to his sister's shame, which would lead him thus to trifle, in a lampoon, with so grave a subject.

The subsequent evils that have come upon the College, can, I think, be all traced to the action of the Board on that occasion, and I more freely state this, as I take part of the blame to myself. I felt that the charges were of so humiliating and degrading a character, that in no other University in this country, or any country at home, whatever the tenure of the office might be, would a Professor be retained who was guilty of such conduct. He was not acquitted of any one of the charges, and I feel persuaded that there was not one who heard the evidence who was not convinced that they were true. The great evil consisted in giving a second threat after the former caution. This was a weakness which has proved most disastrous to the interests of the

Colleg
assume
After t
mind,.
said he
he had
by son
do not
able c
dentin

It
strato
the ch
some r
have a

Th
1862.
amalgr
entere
likely
numbe
friend
led to
he too
ence i
lieve tl
great c
to the
and m
arrival
langur
denco
close r
the un
ing wi

T
spring
to be
into tl
college
Profe
for th
could

73

College. Professor Weir interpreted our leniency into weakness and cowardice, and he at once assumed an attitude of defiance and insubordination that he never before ventured to assume. After the decision I asked him to call upon me that I might bring him to a peaceful frame of mind, and to work harmoniously with myself and colleagues. He spurned my advances. He said he would live to humble Mr. Paton, and in the way of threat towards myself, he declared that he had means of knowing every word that fell from me in the Board of Trustees, and certainly by some means I- new every word that was uttered here, and every word that was penned. I do not say that that should be a secret Board, but still we have occasion to exercise our honorable confidence in one another. But such honor has not been observed, and the most confidential statements were instantly carried to him.

It will be in the recollection of two fellow Trustees, that when deputed to visit and remonstrate with Professor Weir, about the time of his trial, that I made the remark that he had all the character of insanity, and that the danger was, that when Dr. George left he would fasten on some new victims, and find charges just as grave to bring against them. I could not, however, have anticipated that this prophecy should be fulfilled as it has subsequently been.

The first open attempt at public injury to the College was in the following summer, that of 1862. This was the breaking up of the Grammar School. I had greatly interested myself in amalgamating the College School with the Grammar School, and the leading men of the city heartily entered into the scheme. The advantages to the College promised to be very great, as it was likely to prove an important nursery. And at first the success was beyond all expectation. The numbers were almost doubled, the highest number being 101. Professor Weir was the intimate friend of the Master, Mr. May, and I have no doubt that it was by his influence Mr. May was led to break up the Grammar School, and establish a school of his own. But we are not concerned so much with any private advice he may have given, as the open measures which he took to promote the ruin of the Grammar School. This was done by using his influence in favor of Mr. May in various ways, which had the effect of leading the people to believe that Mr. May represented the interests of the College, and consequently a large proportion of the scholars went with him. Thus the scholars who had been collected for many years, at great expense by the College, were carried off and put under a master who was in open hostility to the College. This hostility was shown in the most marked manner when Professor Murray and myself arrived in the fall of 1862. The students resolved to meet us at the steamer on our arrival, but Mr. May attended the meeting of students called for this purpose, and with violent language strongly dissuaded the students from showing this mark of courtesy. I have no evidence to show what part Mr. Weir took in the matter, but from his well-known feelings, and his close and constant intimacy, it was universally felt that it was agreeable to him, and sprang from the unhappy state of feeling which he had excited. This was the commencement of a tampering with the students which has gone such a length as to destroy the discipline of the College.

The next cases of insubordination are in connection with the drawing up of the Statutes. In the spring of 1862, a committee, of which I was convener, was appointed to draft a code of Statutes, to be submitted to the Trustees, and while in Scotland I occupied much of my time in enquiring into the Constitution and Laws of the Home Universities as well as those of America, and had collected materials for this code. When I returned, I found that Mr. Weir and others of the Professors who were here during the summer, had applied to the Trustees to draw up By-Laws for the Senate; and permission was granted, under the impression that they were not laws that could interfere with the Statutes of the University. To my astonishment I found that Mr.

Weir, and those associated with him, had assumed the functions of the Board of Trustees, had drawn up Statutes of the University, and instead of the Governors defining the powers of the Senate according to the Charter, the Senate defined and limited the power of the Board; and, in particular, the Statutes were directed to the entailment of the Principal's power. These By-Laws were drawn up in the handwriting of Professor Weir, and, from the tenor of them, they were evidently inspired by his feelings. These By-Laws, of course, put the Trustees in a false position, and we were obliged to appear in antagonism to the Senate, seeing that we could not possibly sanction them. Most of the Professors would never, I believe, have taken any hand in these By-Laws if they had been aware that a Committee had been appointed by the Trustees to draw up a code of Statutes. The code of Statutes was drawn up and presented to a general meeting of the Trustees, in the session 1862-63, and after various changes they were adopted in the form in which they are now printed. It was a trying time to draw up Statutes. A time of peace would have been preferable, but it was impossible in the circumstances to delay. Mr. Weir's code of Statutes was thus rejected, and one of a different kind was adopted. Immediately on the passing of the Statutes, the most bitter opposition to them was raised by Mr. Weir.

The first indication was a scandalous and threatening anonymous letter addressed to myself. There was internal evidence to indicate clearly from what quarter it came. I think it was intended that I should understand from whence it came, while, at the same time, there was no legal proof. It contained also extracts of the most scurrilous kind from the *Argus*, against myself and other Trustees. These printed extracts were posted in every part of the town, and one was posted on my desk, in the Chapel, on Sabbath morning, so that when I came in I might see it. I made no attempt to obtain direct evidence that these libels emanated from Professor Weir. I had no doubt in my own mind that directly or indirectly they came from him.

The next case is still worse. About midnight the College was broken into, apparently by a person well acquainted with it. The person must have been possessed with a paint brush and cardboards, with opprobrious names against myself cut out in it. With the brush and card the walls of the College, outside and in, were defaced. The moment it occurred, no one doubted from what quarter it emanated. A Police officer was employed to detect the culprit, and the students of Divinity were on the point of sending for a detective to Montreal, but we did not succeed in finding any clue to the perpetrator. Strong suspicion rested upon a Student of Divinity as the person employed to perpetrate the deed, which makes the case still more atrocious, showing how far the animosity had been carried, when even a Student of Divinity was seduced from his duty to perpetrate the deed. And it is still more lamentable from the fact that if it was a Student of Divinity, he must have been guilty of the deepest hypocrisy, for all the students, without exception, showed outwardly the utmost courtesy and respect. Although this cannot be traced by positive evidence to Professor Weir, no one can have the slightest doubt that it originated from the strife kept up by him.

We have heard so much about the Statutes lately, that at first it might be thought these Statutes were the cause of the strife that exists. This is far from being the case, the animosity was just as intense before, but the Statutes were taken advantage of to feed the flame. The well-affected Professors, who were at first led to ask a modification of the Statutes, have now seen that the agitation about the Statutes was simply a continuance of the strife which has now raged for ten long years.

The following are marked cases of insubordination on Professor Weir's part. During his illness in the session of 1862-3, I called upon him to say that I was ready to provide for the

teaching of his classes, which had been for a considerable time idle. He positively refused, and for several weeks there was no teaching.

Another case of subordination was in reference to the office of Superintendent of the Common School. We have a Statute to the effect that no Professor is entitled to engage in any vocation which the Board shall deem inconsistent with his office. The Trustees gave intimation that they considered this office, in his case, inconsistent with his Professorship, and required him to resign. This he refused to do. The question with us at present is not was the office inconsistent with his Professorship. We have only to do with the fact that it was deemed inconsistent by the Trustees, and that he refused to obey their commands. I do not think that generally the office of Superintendent would be injurious to the College when combined with a Professorship; but certainly in his case it had the most injurious effect, for his position enabled him to injure seriously the College. All his efforts have been directed to injure the system of Scholarships from the Common Schools to the Grammar School, and his position as Superintendent enabled him to do this most effectually. This office, which might be made beneficial to the College, was employed to injure its interests.

Dr. Lawson's removal was made the occasion of uproar and insubordination in the College. The ten years' strife could not fail to form parties in the College, and Mr. Weir, by constantly keeping up agitation, did not fail to form a party who always acted in concert. There were other Professors who always acted along with him, and one of these was Dr. Lawson. On accepting a Professorship in Dalhousie College, he seized the opportunity of declaiming against the Statutes and the Trustees before his students. This caused great excitement among them. The Trustees felt bound to summon him before them, in order that he might be censured for his conduct. This was the occasion of much indignation on the part of Professor Weir and his friends, and the opportunity was taken of manifesting it at a meeting in the Convocation Hall, for the purpose of presenting an address to Dr. Lawson. Not anticipating the results of the meeting, some of the well-affected Professors attended; the speeches of Professor Weir and his friends were of the most inflammatory kind. The Trustees, the Statutes, and the Officers of the College were referred to in a disrespectful manner. One of Professor Weir's statements was, that the Statutes were specially intended for himself. As might be expected, a scene of riot and confusion, which has been rarely paralleled in the history of any University, took place.

A Committee was appointed at the above meeting, of which Mr. May was convener, to draw up a Report of the proceedings. This Report was so scandalous, that THE GLOBE newspaper did not venture to print it. A leading article, however, was founded on the Report most damaging to the interests of the College, full of gross misrepresentations, and to persons unacquainted with the real state of matters, the Governors must have appeared as altogether unworthy of their trust, and the College unworthy of the confidence of the country. I was, personally, the object of bitter remark and misrepresentation. I cannot trace the article directly to Professor Weir, but there can be no doubt it can be traced to the strife which he has stirred up. I have discovered traces of ingenious animosity in circulating this article. It was sent for publication in the newspapers of the Lower Provinces, where I had made a tour during the summer in the service of the Church and College. It was evidently intended to neutralize any good my visit might have done. Professor Weir exultingly showed to one of the Trustees a copy of a New York paper in which the article was inserted. But by far the most injurious step was the insertion of the article in the Scottish newspapers, especially in the newspapers of the Church, and those connected with the locality of my late parish. The Church of Scotland, on whose support we so much depend, has had this laid before it; a picture of our College, showing that it is entirely

19

his al

Dear

I
but f
office
from
say w
defou
slate.
have
Scotl
north

so w
guar
held
late
thro
were
ing

man
own
othe

com
amp

unworthy of the support received by us. In the case of one of the newspapers of Kingston, by ingenious misrepresentations, he stirred up the editor to write in a hostile manner against the Trustees, and myself individually. The editor having detected the misrepresentations, withdrew his statements. On doing so, Professor Weir addressed to him the following letter:

QUEEN'S COLLEGE, KINGSTON, 27th October, 1863.

(To the Editor of the British Whig.)

DEAR SIR,—

In your article of last night's issue, regarding Queen's College, you say—"It is, however, but fair to state that none of the other Professors have given up any permanent income to take office in Canada." I am curious to know whence you got this information. It must have come from one very ill-informed about the antecedents of the Professors in Queen's College. I cannot say whether your statem—as true or false in regard to all my Colleagues. They are able to defend themselves, and may possibly do so. I can only give a public contradiction to your statement as regards myself. *I did give up a permanent income to take office in Canada*, and as I have still in my possession an extract-minute of my appointment to the office which I held in Scotland, I am prepared to convince any one, who is at all sceptical on the subject, that my assertion is correct.

In this respect, then, I stand on a par with Principal Leitch. It is true that I was neither so worldly wise, nor so suspicious of the Trustees of Queen's College, as to extort from them guarantees for the permanency of my office in their Institution; though, like Dr. Leitch, I too held my office in Scotland at the close of my first session in Canada. I had been assured by the late Allen Menzies, Esq., W. S., and Professor of Conveyancing, &c., in Edinburgh University, through whom I was induced to come to Canada, that the Professorships in Queen's College were permanent or life appointments, and so also they have always been regarded, till the framing of the new Statutes lately.

But, Sir, had I taken advantage of my position to render my own situation secure and permanent, I would have heartily despised myself, as unworthy of my race, had I likewise used my own security to degrade my Colleagues, and render their positions insecure. There are several other erroneous statements in your article, with which I shall leave others to deal.

I am, dear Sir, yours truly,

GEORGE WEIR, M. A.,
Professor of Classical Literature,
Queen's College.

Whether such a letter, containing such aspersions and insinuations against the Principal, and coming from a Professor, is consistent with the good government of a College, or a proper example to the students, I leave to the judgment of the Trustees.

About the same time a scurrilous lampoon was circulated in the City against Mr. Paton, Professor Murray and myself. I cannot trace this to Professor Weir, but it was much of the

same style and character with that against Dr. George, to which I have already alluded. Articles evidently from the same source, and of the same character, were published in the *Grumbler* newspaper.

At a meeting of the Senatus, when the conduct of Dr. Lawson was brought under consideration, Professor Weir acted in the most violent manner, and used insulting language towards myself. He was guilty of insubordination in refusing to summon a meeting at the time I, as Chairman, requested him to do so, and called a meeting without any authority, at a time most convenient for some movement in reference to Dr. Lawson. He was further guilty of insubordination in refusing, at a late meeting of Senatus, to insert the name of Mr. Bell in the Sederunt, on the ground that the Statutes were illegal which gave Mr. Bell a seat at the Board.

Again, the matter of the Grammar School has been brought up. Mr. May was recently obliged to leave from parents withdrawing their children ; not, I believe, from any want of confidence in his talents, but from the discredit his connection with Mr. Weir cast upon the school. His departure was again the occasion of Mr. Weir's organizing an opposition to the Grammar School.

MR. BELL'S APPOINTMENT.

It was Mr. Bell's appointment that brought matters to a crisis, and required a general meeting to be held now, instead of at the end of the Session. Hitherto Mr. Weir, and those who acted with him, had succeeded only in stirring up the students to occasional outbreaks ; but they at last succeeded in producing, in the Medical Faculty, a state of chronic disturbance ; and I may mention in passing, that the Arts and Theological students have, so far as known to me, all acted with marked propriety ; and it is proper also to state, that the Divinity Hall had not met when the riotous meeting was held in the Convocation Hall, so that none of the Divinity Students are implicated. Whatever may be the secret influence on the minds of the Arts and Theological students, there has been no known breach of the laws of the College. The recent disturbances have been all in the Medical Faculty, and even there only a few are implicated, but these few have been sufficient to keep, for some time, Mr. Bell's class in a state of disorder. The opposition to Mr. Bell's appointment is readily understood. It is generally believed that Dr. Lawson's resignation was merely a plan of Mr. Weir, and his friends, to compel the Trustees to rescind the Statutes, and so give him a triumph. It was imagined that Dr. Lawson's loss would be fatal to the College, and that rather than lose him, we would undo our own Statutes. Mr. Weir, in order to show how hopeless our case was, stated to one of my colleagues that Dr. Lawson was to write home to Dr. Balfour not to recommend any one to the chair. No ordinary disappointment must therefore, have been felt, when Dr. Lawson's resignation was at once and gladly accepted ; and when, in addition, a Lecturer, certainly not of less talent or promise, was at once appointed. The College has not only benefitted by the change, but Mr. Weir lost by far the most influential member of his party. It was to frustrate such a result, that means were taken to stir up the students against Mr. Bell. As I understand Mr. Bell intends giving an account of the manner in which Mr. Weir and his party effected their object, I shall not enter upon this subject. It is not surprising that students should be tempted to act in a disorderly manner in Mr. Bell's class, when assured that this would be agreeable to some of their Professors. Of this I am convinced, that no man could have done better than Mr. Bell, and that just in proportion to his merits would be the opposition raised against him. I have frequently attended his Lectures in the Arts department, when perfect order was kept. Though so young, he has already given the most gratifying evidence of his future eminence as a lecturer and man of science. He

78

... stood the ordeal through which he has passed most nobly, and has given ample evidence that he will prove loyal to the constitution and government of the College, if permanently appointed.

Among the six members of the Senatus, there is, with one exception, no diversity of opinion as to the serious injury Professor Weir has done the College, and the hopelessness of the College prospering while he remains one of its officers. To this conviction, these members will give their testimony if required to do so.

Among the deplorable results of this state of affairs which I have detailed, I need only mention a few in which its injurious influence may be clearly recognized.

1. The College has seriously lost in its reputation for order and discipline, which are among the most essential elements of the good name of an Educational Institution. In order to retard and check this injury, prompt measures must at once be taken.

2. As might naturally have been expected, students will not attend. Many instances of this have come under my own personal notice. The consequence is, that while other Colleges are advancing rapidly, our own remains stationary. While matters remain as at present, would even a Trustee willingly send a son to Queen's College.

3. The same causes totally unfit our College from discharging what has always been regarded as its main function, that is, of a seminary for the holy ministry of our Church. It is humiliating to confess that no College could at present, as far as the Arts Faculty is concerned, serve the Church's purpose worse than its own.

4. It cannot be matter of surprise that the Bursary Scheme of our Church should droop under such influences, nor that congregations who know how unfit our College is becoming to train young minds to the Holy ministry, should be averse to contributing to its support.

5. Nor must we wonder if the Church at Home should refuse to aid us when they see us incapable of putting down such flagrant and scandalous evils.

6. A Government which, at the best, is not most friendly, will have no difficulty in finding in a or state of the College, a sufficient pretext for withdrawing its grant.

7. The state of my health will render it a physical impossibility for me to continue to discharge my duties unless peace and good government can be restored.

8. There are brightening prospects before us, and much may yet be made of the excellent elements within the College if only we take a firm stand at the present moment. But all the elements are powerless for good while matters remain in their present unsatisfactory position.

"W."

Referred to in the evidence of John Clark Murray.

See article No. 10 of documents produced by Plaintiff under order for production.

of (
pro
Woo

from
to th
Supe
prov
fesso
by M

Woo

79

" X. "

Referred to in the evidence of John Clark Murray.

Some of the cases of Impropriety with the names of those who can substantiate them.

1. Strife with Professor Smith, can be proved by Trustees of that period.

2. *First* quarrel with Dr. George, when brought before the Board, can be proved by Trustees of that period.

3. *Second* quarrel with Dr. George,—when brought before Trustees and cautioned—can be proved by Trustees at that Meeting.

The cases will be given in detail hereafter.

4. Endeavouring to injure the Grammar School—can be proved by Local Trustees, C. M. Woods.

5. Encouraging disobedience to the Statutes—can be proved by the Professors.

6. Consequences of Professor Weir's conduct, in the shape of posting of Bills and Extracts from the *Argus* newspaper—can be proved by Professors and Trustees.

7. Breaking into the College and defacing its walls with scandalous inscriptions, attributable to the same causes—can be proved by the Professors.

8. Insubordination in not obeying the requirement of the Trustees to give up the office of Superintendent of Schools—can be proved by Local Trustees.

9. Insubordination in not permitting his classes to be taught during his illness—can be proved by Professor Murray.

10. Factious opposition to Campbell Scholarship and its provisions—can be proved by Professors Murray and Mowat.

11. Stirring up Editor of *Whig* newspaper to write calumnious articles—can be proved by Mr. Paton and Editor's Letter.

12. The letter in the *Whig* directed against me—can be proved by the Letter itself.

13. Turbulent conduct at Meeting in Convocation Hall—can be proved by Dr. Yates, Mr. Woods, and Medical Students generally.

20

tules

and j
agem

1
1
spoke

I
To th

Dear

I
meeth
making

I
Weir

14. Insulting conduct towards me in Senatus—can be proved by Professors Murray and Mowat.

15. Summoning a meeting of Senatus without authority—can be proved by Professors Murray and Mowat.

16. Refusing to insert Mr. Bell's name in Sederunt, on the alleged ground that the Statutes were illegal—can be proved by Professor Murray.

17. Calumnious charges contained in Lampoons in the *Globe* and *Grumbler* newspapers, and in anonymous Letters, attributable to the conduct of Professor Weir, if not to his direct agency or procurement.

18. Opposition to Mr. Bell's appointment.

19. His general conduct as being highly injurious to the welfare of the College—can be spoken to by Professors Murray, Mowat and Bell.

" A. A. "

Referred to in the evidence of Wm. Ireland.

To the Hon. John Hamilton,
    Chairman of the Board of Trustees of Queen's College.

DEAR SIR,—

I am under the painful necessity of requesting that, as soon as convenient, you will call a meeting of the Board to investigate a certain grievous charge which Professor Weir has been making against my moral character.

I have delayed for some time to make this application, from the impression that Professor Weir was about to move in the matter. But I cannot in justice, either to the College or myself, forbear any longer to bring the business before the Board.
    I am, Dear Sir,
        Yours truly,
Kingston, 17th Oct., 1861.   JAMES GEORGE.

" B. B. "

Referred to in the evidence of Wm. Ireland.

DEAR SIR,—   Kingston, Oct. 2nd, 1861.

In answer to yours of the 1st inst., asking for a statement of the charge which Professor Weir has been making against my moral character: I have to say, that on the 9th ult. Professor

Woir
years
the fa

sever.
the B

Mr. ?

I

My D
I
of the
paper
suital
with.

Mr. V

Weir wrote me to this effect—that his sister, who left this country for Scotland about seven years ago, after her return to Scotland gave birth to a child, and in said letter he accuses me as the father of this child.

I have good grounds also for saying that Professor Weir has made the same statement to several persons since his arrival in Canada. This then is the unutterably painful business which the Board will have to take up.

I am, dear Sir,

Yours truly,

JAMES GEORGE.

Mr. William Ireland,
Sec'y to the Board of T. Q. C.

" C. C. "

Referred to in the evidence of Wm. Ireland.

Kingston, Nov. 11th, 1861.

My Dear Sir,—

I have to request that, as Clerk of the Board, you will communicate to me the deliverances of the Board on the 7th as to my business. And I have more especially to ask for copies of all papers or documents which have been tabled or lodged against me, so that I may have suitable opportunity to reply to them. This fair request will, of course, be readily complied with.

I am, dear Sir,

Yours truly,

JAMES GEORGE.

Mr. Wm. Ireland,
Sec'y to the Board of T. Q. C.

" D. D. "

. Referred to in the evidence of Wm. Ireland.

Kingston, Nov. 16th, 1861.

My Dear Sir,—

I thank you for the documents you sent me on the 12th. I am sorry to trouble you, but I would take it kind if you would be so good as send me authenticated and correct copies of the letters referred to in Professor Weir's statement to the Board. I mean copies of my own letters as well as his

I am, my dear Sir,

Yours truly,

JAMES GEORGE.

Mr. William Ireland,
Sec'y to the Board of T. Q. C.

Ref

To
Dear Si
I n
Judge M
sign my
the clos
and pai
also fron
affected.

Ref

WM. Ir

Dear St
Af
Princip
uniform
respectf

Re

Wm. I

Di
George

82

" F. E. "

Referred to in the evidence of Wm. Ireland.

To the Chairman of the Board of Trustees of Queen's College.

DEAR SIR,—

I now state in writing what I stated verbally yesterday to Principal Leitch and Judge McLean, that it is my intention—an intention I have had for more than ten years—to resign my situation as Professor in the College, which I now do, this resignation to take effect at the close of the session. This step I am induced to take more especially from the discomfort and painful feelings I have had in time past in certain matters connected with the College, and also from a peculiar condition of brain affection with which I have been for a considerable time affected.

I am, Dear Sir,
Yours, truly,
JAMES GEORGE.

———

" F. F. "

Referred to in the evidence of Wm. Ireland.

Kingston, 11th December, 1861.

WM. Ireland, Esq.,
Sec'y to Board of Trustees of the University of Queen's College.

DEAR SIR,—

After considering the subject of the interviews which I had with Mr. Justice McLean and the Principal, I have resolved, if need be, to adduce satisfactory evidence in support of my sister's uniform and solemn asseverations that Dr. George is the father of her illegitimate child, and I respectfully request the privilege of appearing before you to make out a prima facie case.

Yours, sincerely,
GEORGE WEIR.

———

" G. G. "

Referred to in the evidence of Wm. Ireland.

Kingston, 11th Dec., 1861.

Wm. Ireland, Esq.,
Sec'y to Board of Trustees of the University of Queen's College.

DEAR SIR,—Would you kindly furnish me with an extract of the Minute regarding Professor George's complaint against me?

Yours, sincerely,
GEORGE WEIR.

My De
I
to my
greatly

Mr. W

Re

WILLIA

Sir,—
I
corresp
of Que
mo aga
me to
made
nature
shown

83

" H. H. "

Referred to in the evidence of Wm. Ireland.

Friday Afternoon.

MY DEAR SIR, -

I will not say that I am anxious to know what the deliverance of the Board was in reference to my business. I expected a communication from you to-day, but none has come. You will greatly oblige me by sending the deliverance this evening, or as soon as you conveniently can.

I am, my dear Sir,

Yours, truly,

Mr. Wm. Ireland,
Sec'y to the Board of Q. C.

JAMES GEORGE.

" I. I."

Referred to in the evidence of William Ireland.

Kingston, 6th November, 1861.

WILLIAM IRELAND, Esq.,
Secretary to the Board of Trustees of the University of Queen's College.

SIR,—

I beg to acknowledge the receipt of your letter of the 31st ultimo, enclosing copies of a correspondence which has taken place between yourself, as Secretary to the Board of Trustees of Queen's College, and Professor George, relating to an imputation said to have been made by me against that gentleman, in a letter addressed by me to him some time since, and calling upon me to "place before the Board, in writing, the charge or accusation which, it appears, I had made against Professor George, and to substantiate same." I beg to say in reply, that the nature of the imputation which I am said to have made against Professor George will best be shown by the correspondence which has passed between us in reference to it, and which I now submit to the Board of Trustees. It is as follows :

Copy of my first letter to Professor George.

Kingston, 31st August, 1861.

PROFESSOR GEORGE :

SIR,—During my visit to Scotland I became acquainted with circumstances which had previously been carefully concealed from me, and which render any—the slightest intercourse with you—impossible. You cannot fail to know what these circumstances are.

I have in consideration, and am taking counsel, both in Scotland and in Canada, how far it is my duty to make these the subject of investigation in the proper quarters.

I am, Sir,

Your obedient servant,

(Signed) GEORGE WEIR.

To which the following reply was received by me on the 2nd September, 1861 :

21

In
not wh
H
bring
" *defr*
but for
the Co
for ye
termin
mind t
chose

Pnote
St
first a
a child
hour o
that yo
the sli

A
plain
before
your c

Kingston, Monday.

Professor Weir:

Sir,—I have to demand an instant and explicit statement, as to what you have learned in Scotland as to me, which renders it impossible for you to hold any intercourse with me.

I am, Sir, yours, &c.,

(Signed,) JAMES GEORGE.

A week from this date, although I had sent no answer to the above, I received the following from him :

Kingston, 9th September, 1861.

Professor Weir :

Sir,—I have waited sufficiently long for an answer to my note of the second, yet I have no answer from you.

In your letter of the 30th ult. you hint at certain steps which you intend to take. I know not what you mean to do.

But in reference to what "tear" the air of a threat, I have merely to say, that if you shall bring any false charges against me injurious to my character, you may rest assured of it I shall "defend" myself to the uttermost—and that, not from a mere regard to my own self-interests, but for what I owe to interests "infinitely" higher than my own. As to my future connection with the College, that is, indeed, to me a small matter. My connection with that Institution has been for years past, on many accounts, so unpleasant and painful, that I have long wished it should terminate, and I have resolved it shall terminate at the close of the ensuing session. But never mind that. Proceed to carry out your threat, if you deem it proper to do so. This, of course, closes my correspondence with you.

I am, Sir, yours, &c.,

(Signed,) JAMES GEORGE.

Copy of my Second letter to Dr. George.

Kingston, 20th September, (not 9th, as in his letter to Secretary of Trustees.) 1861.

Professor George :

Sir,—I think it right to give you now the explicit information which you demanded in your first note to me after my return from Scotland. What I learnt in Scotland was, that my sister bore a child in March 1855—a son—at this moment a living image of yourself, and known from the hour of its birth only by your name—of which child she has uniformly and solemnly affirmed that you are the father. Such being the case, I felt it my duty at once to inform you that any—the slightest intercourse—with you is impossible.

After further and full consideration of the matter, I have made up my mind that it is my plain duty to the Institution with which we are both connected, to prefer a charge against you before the Trustees, for the wrong, the deep, irreparable wrong you have done my sister unless your connection with the College is at once terminated.

85

I am desirous of avoiding publicity, not only for family reasons, but in the interests of the Church and the College; but such a feeling, though natural, must and shall, if need be, yield to the dictates of duty. Should you, therefore, persist in your intention of not retiring from the College untill the end of the session, instead of at once doing so, I shall feel myself obliged to lay the whole matter before the Trustees at once, and also to take such legal proceedings as I may be advised. In such case, there need be no delay in bringing the matter to a conclusion, as my sister's evidence, as also the evidence from documents bearing on the subject, can, as I have ascertained on the best legal authority, be taken in Scotland on written interrogatories, under a Commission. I need in Court here, to substantiate the charge.

I am, Sir,

Your obedient servant,

(Signed.)   GEORGE WEIR.

Copy of Professor George's third letter to me.

Kingston, Thursday evening.

PROFESSOR WEIR,—

SIR,—Your letter of to-day is sufficiently explicit. No, never. I would rather be "*chewn*" to pieces than do what you propose. No, Sir, I am not guilty of what you lay to my charge. If I were, and denied the charge, that were indeed a far greater offence in the sight of God, than even the crime of which I am accused. But you assume my guilt, and wish me to admit. The assumption on your pa... is natural, but it is false.

I will not, however, argue the question with you—that were useless, nor is it needful, as you seem resolved that the matter shall be tried by the competent tribunals. Well be it so, if you think that the ends of justice, and the interests of the College, and of religion, demand it.

I shall give no expression to my feelings in such a letter as this. I shall merely say, that it is indeed a most grave matter, and will assuredly have grave issues, go as it may, if it goes to the public.

I am not insensible as to what you say as to publicity; yet, Sir, I would rather a thousand times have the utmost publicity than secret surmises as to such a charge. Do as you deem right. I have no more to say.

I am, Sir, yours, &c.,

(Signed.)   JAMES GEORGE.

It will be seen by this correspondence, that I contempl... the necessity of bringing the subject of it under the consideration of some competent authority, at some future time, but that I had not indicated the time when, or the tribunal before which I might eventually think it expedient to submit it. I am aware, however, that the Board of Trustees has ample authority for assuming the right of investigating it in the way indicated in your communication, and I cheerfully yield that obedience to their command, which, as a Professor in the College, is proper on my part. It will be necessary, notwithstanding, that sufficient time be given to me to obtain from Scotland, in a proper shape, the evidence which induced me to inform Dr. George that "I could hold no intercourse with him." Upon which communication, when, as yet, I had made no accusation, he predicated that I intended to bring "Charges against him, injurious to his character," and threw out a suggestion that he intended to terminate his connection with the College at the end of the ensuing session.

86

I shall use all diligence to procure this evidence, and shall submit it to the Board of Trustees as soon as I find that I have it in a shape proper for investigation. Several weeks, or perhaps months, must elapse before this can be accomplished, but I beg that you will assure the Board of Trustees that no time will be lost on my part.

I have the honour to be, yours truly,

GEORGE WEIR.

——

"K. K."

Referred to in the evidence of John Paton.

To the Honorable Alexander Campbell.

Queen's College, 4th February, 1864.

Dear Sir,—

I beg to apply to you, as Counsel for Queen's College, for your opinion on the following points :

I am, dear Sir, yours truly,

WILLIAM LEITCH.

1. Have the Board of Trustees of Queen's College power to dismiss a Professor of Queen's College on their own motion, without a complaint.

1. Yes, I am of opinion that the Trustees have this power, subject to general rules mentioned hereafter.

2. If so, what procedure should be adopted, and what if any formalities should be required.

2. The proposal to remove must be considered at a duly convened meeting of the Board, and the dismissal be by resolution, or under seal, (as the appointment was) if the proposed removal be for cause, the meeting of the Trustees must have been duly convened for the purpose of hearing the case, and the accused must be summoned before the Board, and heard in his defence. If the proposed proceeding be to remove at discretion, these formalities may be omitted. A removal without complaint, but for cause, if that cause was a sufficient one, would not entail the payment of any salary after dismissal. A dismissal at discretion, would entail a liability to pay the Professor dismissed compensation by way of damages, unless six months' notice of the intention to dismiss be given him, ending with his year. Six months' salary, or salary to the end of the current year of his engagement, if more than six months of it remained unexpired, would be a reasonable compensation. I think the latter certainly would.

87

3. What grounds will justify such removal?

4. Is there any need for recording such grounds.

5. If, after removing a Professor without a complaint, it was found that such procedure was illegal, would it be competent to institute a new enquiry by complaint in reference to the same charges.

6. On the supposition that a Professor can not be removed without a complaint, is it in the power of the Trustees to modify his salary at pleasure in Chapter XIX.

WILLIAM LEITCH.

3. A Professor of Queen's College is, as such, a ministerial officer of the Corporation, and has no franchise in his office which is not of the essence of the Corporation; he may, I think, be removed from it at the pleasure of the Trustees, subject to the general rules of law affecting all contracts of hiring and service. If dismissed without cause, he is entitled to six months' notice, ending with the year of his engagement, or to compensation in money. I say six months to be on the right side; three might do if his salary was payable quarterly. If the removal is to be for cause then any offence against the duties of his office, or the ruinous interest of the Corporation, incapacity, insubordination, &c., &c., would be sufficient grounds if the auction be the simple exercise of the volition of the Trustees. No grounds are of course necessary, but the Trustees give six months' notice, ending with the year of the engagement, or pay compensation. I do not think the concluding paragraph of the 14th Statute in any way alters the general rules of law as regards contracts made prior to the enactment of the Statutes of 1863.

4. If the proposed proceeding is to be simply an exercise of the discretionary power of the Trustees, I do not think it necessary that the grounds thereof should be recorded. If the proposed proceeding is to be for cause, either upon complaint, or on the mere motion of the Trustees, the grounds should be recorded; in the former case the Charter is imperative.

5. I think it would be competent, in the supposed case put, to try the accused Professor on a complaint under the Charter, and the 14th Statute. His status as Professor, would in that case remain intact, subject to the result of that trial.

6. It could not be modified until the existing contract with such Professor be terminated by a six months' notice, ending with the year of his engagement.

A. CAMPBELL.

Kingston, February 8th, 1864.

It

br
of
pr
fiv
th

por
Co
Pr

nav
mc

tan

di

D,

I
lif
ac
m
M
a
th
fo
le
ye

88

" L. L. "

Referred to in the evidence of James Williamson.

Montreal, 28 February, 1853.

REVEREND PROFESSOR GEORGE, and the other Professors Queen's College.

DEAR SIRS,—

You will be glad, I have no doubt, to learn that the Committee appointed by the Synod have succeeded in effecting a favorable arrangement with the Government, for the commutation of the Ministers' allowances, the nature of it being, that we will be able, without touching the principal, to pay all ministers placed before 9th May, 1853, £112 10s. per annum during their lives or incumbencies. We think also that a satisfactory arrangement will yet be made for those inducted after that period.

One pleasing feature of the bargain is the securing Queen's College of £500 a year in perpetuity; this was done with the consent of the Government, by putting the £500 paid to the College by the Commissioners of the Reserves Fund, as an allowance of £125 to each of the four Professors, and commuting with them for that sum.

For this purpose I enclose the necessary papers to each by mail, and you will please communicate this letter to them in explanation, as the labour connected with this matter is so enormous, I am unable to write a letter to each, which I would otherwise do.

Please let each execute these papers as directed in the circular letter, before witnesses, and make affidavit as to age, and return them to me by mail as early as possible.

I am, my dear Sir,

Yours, sincerely,

HUGH ALLAN.

If anything was to happen the College, the annuity would be paid to the Professors individually.

" I M. "

Referred to in evidence of John C. Murray.

Montreal, 8th January, 1862.

DEAR DR. LEITCH,—

I received your letter in due course, and had been considering the question. On reflection, I do not think that the Board would be justified in limiting its powers by making all its offices life offices, a thing unknown in any other corporation in this country, if no such limitation actually exists. I therefore suggest, as the matter is an important one, that the Executive Committee should submit the case I enclose to the Hon. J. H. Cameron, of Toronto, and Hon. O. Mowat, and obtain their opinion, which would settle the matter with all reasonable men. I hold a strong opinion on the matter myself, and I am satisfied that we would inflict serious injury on the College by surrounding it with perpetual officers. Professors and Janitors stand on the same footing under the Charter. I suppose the course suggested will cost, perhaps £10, and it will be well spent. I cannot promise to be in Kingston on the 27th. I am told that Parliament is to meet on the 31st, and if so, I will have much to do in preparing to leave home. In some matters you had better select your own time, and *I will come if I can*. I find I could not now be absent after the 24th. Perhaps, if there is no urgent necessity the Statutes might be printed, distributed,

and lie over for a time. But I do not think you will meet with any difficulty in having a code passed such as you may prepare.

Reciprocating your kind wishes, and regretting my inability to meet your views,

Yours, truly,

(Signed), A. MORRIS.

" 2 M. "

Referred to in the evidence of John C. Murray.

Quebec, 28th September, 1863.

MY DEAR SIR,—

As I find I cannot attend the meeting of the Board of Trustees relative to the Statutes, I now write you to explain my views.

I am quite prepared to assume the responsibility for the Statutes, (16, referring to the Professors as I suggested it. It is taken, in effect, from the McGill College Statutes, and is, so far as I know, the general rule in force in Canada. I do not, however, understand that it is retroactive in its action, but I believe it in effect states the actual position of the Professors relative to the Trustees. Still, as the rule for the future is a good one, there would be no objection to a proviso declaring that the Statute is not retroactive.

I hold strongly by the Statutes 13 and 14. The last simply declares the incidental power which the Trustees, as Governors, employ of dealing with their officers on their own motion and authority. The 13th provides for the action to be taken in the case of a Professor, Student or member of the Church applying to the Board for redress as against an officer.

The Board have the opinion of the Hon. A. Campbell in favor of the incidental power of the Board, and I hope they will not surrender it.

Some of the amendments sought are not of much importance, and others may be dealt with in a conciliatory spirit, but there is a disposition to magnify the powers of the Senate.

Let it be borne in mind that the Charter creates the Senate a Court for the exercise of academical superintendence and discipline over the Students, &c., but " with such powers for maintaining order and enforcing obedience to the Statutes, Rules and Ordinances *as to the said Board may seem meet and necessary.*" Clause 22.—It is for the Board to say what powers it chooses to give the Senate for the purposes the Court of the Senate was intended to effect. The simple fact is, the Trustees are the Governors, and the Senate are subordinate to them, and the sooner the relative position of parties is understood, the better it will be for the institution.

Yours, truly,

Signed, A. MORRIS.

" 3 M. "

Referred to in the evidence of John C. Murray.

Quebec, 25th September, 1865.

MY DEAR SIR, -

I have yours of the 22nd, and am glad to learn that your trip was so pleasant.

I had laid aside the papers re the College for perusal at a quiet moment, which has never

come. My attendance will be contingent upon my duties here. Mr. Allan is willing to attend, and he is quite a match for Judge Malloch; drop him a note on the subject.

I have had two long letters from Dr. Urquhart, but have not had leisure yet to reply to him. I will write you again when I can see my way a little more clearly.

I enclose you a letter from Paton in the subject of the Mission, with two notes from Professor Mitchell.

Perhaps you had better hold a meeting of the Executive.

————

"4 M."

Referred to in the evidence of John C. Murray.

"Time to be agreed on":

Provided, however, that tenure of any office to which appointment was made prior to the 20th day of January, 1863, shall be regulated and governed by the terms of such appointment, and the nature of the understanding and agreement in regard thereto.

Or more simply—

All officers *to be hereafter appointed* shall have their duties, &c.

————

"5 M."

Referred to in the evidence of John C. Murray.

[*Private.*]

Kingston, Canada, 13th Sept., 1861.

My Dear Sir:

I hasten to acknowledge receipt of your official reply to the Resolutions of the Board, also the kind private letter accompanying it, and two letters received previously.

We now understand perfectly your views and wishes, and I lose no time in stating that your conditions will be granted purely and simply, and the requisite resolution forwarded by the Canadian steamer leaving Quebec on the 21st inst.

Previous to the meeting on 8th August, both Mr. Hamilton and myself firmly believed that the conditions in your letter would be granted. We saw and obtained the consent of more than a majority of the Trustees, but, unfortunately, the Trustees whom we saw were so confident that this would be done at once, that they did not deem it necessary to attend the meeting. I think I explained to you that at the meeting Judge Malloch opposed the granting of the conditions strongly, in which he was joined by Dr. Urquhart, and, in addition to this difficulty, we were of opinion that you would be satisfied with the Resolutions sent, which seemed to embrace all that was needed. It was in this way that the conditions—especially No. 4, the most important one—were not agreed to as they stand.

On Friday, the 20th instant, an adjourned special meeting is to be held here; and we now have the assurance of a majority of the Board that they will attend and approve the *five* conditions named by you. Mr. Hamilton went down to Montreal this morning, and I go up to Toronto and Hamilton this evening, where we will see the Trustees, and get, not only their consent that was given before to your conditions, but also their promise to come down to the

meeting. In addition to this, I may also state that Dr. Machar has just come up from Montreal, and that while there he saw Drs. Cook and Mathieson, Messrs. Morris and Allan ; and that all of them, including himself, at once decided that all you desire should be conceded.

My reasons for giving you these details is to show that you can now make your preparations for leaving. Every day is of the utmost importance, and we hope to welcome you back as soon as you possibly can get away from Scotland.

Had we understood, as well as we now do, your decision and views, all this delay would not have occurred. Some of the Trustees regard your office as held at pleasure of the Board, and the argument used at last meeting was, that you held your office on the same tenure, or, at least, quite as firmly as any Minister. Now, however, that your difficulty is known, it will be at once set at rest. Our first Resolution embraced all that you required, and applied to all sources of revenue, except fees.   *   *   *   *   *

Very truly yours,

Rev. Dr. Leitch.   JOHN PATON.

———

" 6 M."

Referred to in the evidence of John C. Murray.

Montreal, 1st August, 1861.

DEAR DR. LEITCH :

I take advantage of a moment of comparative leisure to write you in relation to your last favour. In the event of the Trustees acceding, which is likely, to your proposal, I think you ought at once to feel that you are the permanent Principal, and resign your charge. As long as you hold it you will not feel permanent. We always regarded it as a permanent appointment. A special meeting of Trustees is called for next Thursday to consider your letter.   *   *   *   *

Faithfully yours,

A. MORRIS.

———

" 7 M."

Referred to in the evidence of John C. Murray.

Toronto, 5th August, 1861.

MY DEAR SIR,—

Mr. Paton informed of your having written to him, expressing some desire to have an assurance that your situation in Queen's College would be a permanent one, in the event of a union being brought about between the several branches of the Presbyterian Church in Canada. Now, I must confess that I never imagined that there was, or could be, any question on that point. The Trustees of Queen's College, under the direction of the Synod, never could have supposed that any gentleman, competent to fill the situation of Principal of Queen's College, could be expected to leave a permanent provision, and forsake his own country and friends, upon

23

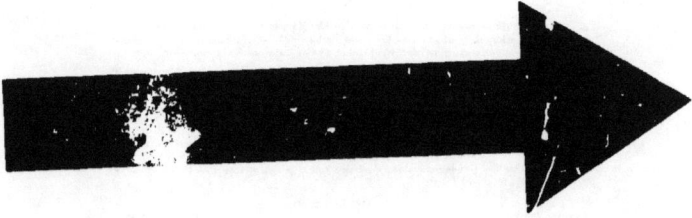

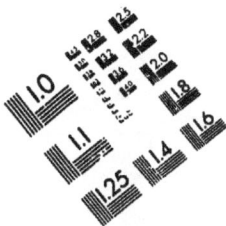

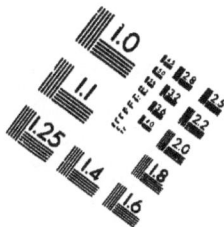

**IMAGE EVALUATION
TEST TARGET (MT-3)**

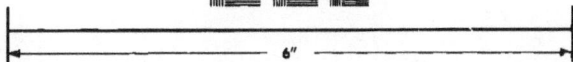

6"

Photographic
Sciences
Corporation

23 WEST MAIN STREET
WEBSTER, N.Y. 14580
(716) 872-4503

the chance of being retained in office here for an uncertain period, depending on some contingency which might be brought about, but which was not even thought of when you consented to accept the proposition made to you. I am only surprised now that a doubt could have suggested itself to you on the subject, and must think that some kind friend who is anxious to retain you as the occupant of Monimail Manse, or some other pleasant residence in your "ain kintry," has started the doubt for the purpose of showing the greater certainty of your position in Scotland than in Canada.

We thought that after some trials and disappointments we had at last got a Principal whose heart would be in his work, and from all we have seen and heard, are not likely to be disappointed. It is not, therefore, very probable that, even for the sake of Church Union, Queen's College will be placed in jeopardy. A union may take place, but in all probability at a distant day ; there are many obstacles in the way, but this you may rely upon, that Queen's College will not be left to the tender mercies of parties who know nothing about it, or who may have their feelings engaged in favor of a *sickly* institution of their own. The present Presbyterian Church of Canada, as it has been called, I strongly suspect, would be delighted to have Queen's College instead of Knox's. If ever a union does take place, the Principal of Queen's College will have no reason to fear that his situation will be injuriously affected in any way. I shall be happy to see you back in the Autumn, as contemplated when we parted at Kingston. In the meantime, allow me to wish you much pleasure among your friends.

I am, my dear Sir,

Yours, very truly,

(Signed.)   A. McLEAN.

REV. PRINCIPAL LEITCH,

      Monimail Manse, Ladybank, Scotland.

" S M. "

Referred to in the evidence of John C. Murray.

Queen's College, Kingston, Canada, 9th August, 1861.

MY DEAR DR. LEITCH,—

Enclosed you will receive a copy of certain Resolutions adopted at a very full meeting of the Board of Trustees, this day, in reply to your letter of the 10th July.

As I write within a few minutes of the close of the mail, I cannot enter into explanations at such length as I would otherwise have done, but I cannot allow the enclosed to be sent off without assuring you that these Resolutions met with the unanimous and cordial concurrence of the Trustees present, and I have good reason to believe would also meet with the hearty approval of those absent.

I am instructed to state that the Board never contemplated the reduction of the salary of the Principal, and would not now have referred to it *but for the reference* in your own letter ; and with regard to the permanency of your position as the Principal of the College, the Board have the strongest conviction that nothing likely to arise in the history of the Province could render it precarious.

Earnestly hoping that the reply of the Trustees will prove satisfactory to you, and will relievo your mind from all anxiety or doubt with regard to the security of your appointment as Principal, and looking forward with pleasure to your return in due time amongst us,

I remain,

My dear Dr. Leitch,

Yours, very respectfully,

(Signed,)   JNO. HAMILTON,

Chairman of the Board.

To the Rev. Dr. Leitch,

Principal of Queen's College, &c., &c.

"O M."

Referred to in the evidence of John C. Murray.

CASE.

The Charter of the Queen's College gave to the Trustees "full power and authority to elect "and appoint, for the said College, a Principal, who shall be a Minister of the Church of Scot-"land, or of the Presbyterian Church of Canada in connection with the Church of Scotland; "and such Professor or Professors, Master or Masters, Tutor or Tutors, and such other officer or "officers as to the said Trustees shall seem meet." (Vide Charter.)

A subsequent clause provides, that if any complaint respecting the conduct of the Principal or any Professor, Master, Tutor, or other Officer of the said College, be at any time made to the Board of Trustees, they may institute an enquiry, and in the event of any impropriety of conduct being duly proved, they shall admonish, reprove, suspend, or remove the person offending as to them may seem good: provided always that the grounds of such admonition, reproof, suspension or removal be recorded at length in the Books of the said Board.

Difference of opinion having arisen as to the powers of the Board with regard to removal from office, and the nature of the appointments thereto, advice of Counsel is sought on the following points:

QUESTIONS.

1. Have the Board the power, under the Charter, of making appointments to Professorships and other offices "during pleasure," as the appointments in the Canadian Colleges are ordinarily made, or upon such such other terms as they may agree upon with the individuals appointed, or are the appointments made by the Board necessarily life appointments?

2. Have the Board the ordinary power incidental to Corporations generally, of the removal from the appointment of Professor, and other officers, for insubordination, incompetency, or other good reason, and that without the necessity of a "complaint"; or is the provision as to a complaint in any way limitative of the power of removal?

3. Does the complaint referred to in the Statute not chiefly refer to complaints made by Professors, Students and others, against officers, rather than to action by the Trustees of their own motion against such officers, under their general powers as Trustees of the Corporation? May the Trustees, of their own motion, remove without any judicial enquiry or proof?

4. What is the nature of the proof of impropriety of conduct contemplated by the Charter by the words "duly proved," and must such proof be on oath, and how ought it to be received and taken?

5. Should it be held that the Principal and Professors, when appointed simply on the terms of the Charter, enjoy a life tenure, and can not be removed except by the judicial process laid down in the Charter. Will the same hold in respect to Lecturers, Tutors, Secretaries, Librarians, Janitors, &c.; or does the circumstance that a quorum of Thirteen is required for removal only in the case of a Principal or a Professor, indicate that the above subordinate officers hold their office only during the pleasure of the Board.

" 10 M. "

Referred to in the evidence of John C. Murray.

The University, Kingston, C. W.,

186 .

My Dear Sir,—

I have directed the Janitor to get your former opinion from the Secretary, Mr. Ireland. One object of the enquiries is to know whether we can make a Statute to the following effect :

"All officers, except in cases provided for by special engagement, shall hold their appointment only during the pleasure of the Board."

And in regard to removal, the following—"That officers may be removed in two ways : 1st, by complaint. In such the Board shall act judicially. The complainer to be prosecutor, and the charges to be duly proved and recorded ; or 2nd, by the Board taking up the case of their own motion, without a complaint, and without judicial proof, or any record of the grounds of removal simply animating the removal, as in the case of any other Corporation."

The above mode of removal is, I think, in harmony with your former opinion.

I think your opinion is consistent with common sense. The Institution would be quite unworkable if the Janitor, Librarian, Secretaries, &c., could not be removed without a judicial process, from which there might be an appeal to the civil Courts.

I remain,

Yours, very truly,

(Signed,)   W. LEITCH

If you tell the bearer when to go back for your answer, he will do so. If we recorded the ground of removal, say theft, without a judicial process of proof, would we not be liable to a libel for damages?"

"11 M."

Referred to in the evidence of John C. Murray.

Toronto, 15th January, 1863.

My Dear Sir,—

I send herewith a form of summons to be used in all cases of complaints, requiring an answer to be filed within a certain time in the office of the Secretary of the Board of Trustees, and then notifying and requiring the party to appear in person to answer the matters of complaint at some other day to be named. You will see that, in order to give as much weight as possible, I propose that the summons shall be under the *seal* of the University, and to be signed by the President and Secretary of the Board of Trustees. I most sincerely hope there may be no occasion for enquiry into the conduct of any one connected with the University, but should there be any such, it will be well to be able to point to an *established rule*, by which the proceedings *must* be heard. No *letters*, from or to individuals, will then be put forward as the *accusation and the proof*, and no person will whisper a word of complaint without being prepared to become prosecutor. I have been engaged for some time as a member of a Commission, which sits twice a year in this place, to investigate claims of persons entitled to land as heirs, devisees or assignees of deceased persons, who purchased or derived title immediately from the Crown. The sittings will close to-morrow.

With united best regards, and that He who rules the seasons may leave many happy returns in store for you, is the earnest wish of,

Dear Sir,

Yours, very truly,

The Rev. Dr. Leitch,—   (Signed,)   A. McLEAN.
Queen's College, Kingston.

"12 M."

Referred to in the evidence of John C. Murray.

To A. B., ————, of ————, in the City of Kingston, Principal or Professor (as the case may be) in the University of Queen's College, Kingston.

Whereas, a complaint hath been duly entered, in writing, against you, as such Principal or Professor, before the Board of Trustees of the said University, of which a true copy is hereunto annexed; and *whereas*, the said Board hath resolved that the matters contained in the said complaint shall be further enquired into and adjudicated upon ; you are, therefore, hereby required to file, in the office of the Secretary of the said Board, at the said University, within ———— days after the service hereof, your answer to the matters in the said complaint contained, and you are hereby notified and required to be and appear, in your proper person, before the said Board, at a meeting to be held at the said University, on ————, the ———— day of ———— next, in order to your defence in the said matters of complaint.

In witness whereof, the Seal of the said University is hereto affixed.

(Signed,)   W. IRELAND,   (Signed,   J. HAMILTON,
   Secretary Queen's College.   Chairman Board of Trustees.

"14 M."

Referred to in the evidence of John C. Murray.

Montreal, 3rd February, 1864.

Dear Paton :

I duly received your last letter, and arranged with Allan and Mr. Hamilton to attend the adjourned meeting. I think it might have been well to have had a complaint based on the

24

letter to "*The Whig*," and the acting as School Inspector, on account of insubordination But I would advise, if the intention is to remove him, to place the whole matter before Mr. Campbell, and have a written opinion from him, which can be read at the meeting, or to the Board of Trustees, to dismiss on the incidental powers, al defining the procedure.

Whether Weir be summoned before the Board, or how he would suggest to act.

The Senate ought to put down insubordination among the students. I will try and prevail upon Allan to leave on Monday evening, so as to give us Tuesday to consult.

Yours truly,

A. MORRIS.

P. S.—I would issue the customary circular from the Secretary of the adjourned meeting, to prevent any pleading cognizance of the actual adjournment. Let it cover all competent business.

I think Campbell has given an opinion already, but one in answer to the queries I enclose will justify your action and strengthen your hands at the Board. Weir will, doubtless, resort to law; therefore the need for precau

---

EXH. F No. 1.

Referred to in the examination of Plaintiff taken at Kingston 21st September, 1861.

University of Queen's College.

COPY OF THE TRUSTEE'S DECISION IN THE CASE OF DR. GEORGE.

Extract from the proceedings at a meeting of the Board of Trustees of the University of Queen's College, Kingston, held in the College on the 12th day of December, 1861.

Moved by Mr. Allan, seconded by Mr. Cameron, as follows:

"The Trustees having received from Dr. George the resignation of his situation of Professor "in the College, to take effect at the end of the present Session, on the ground of ill health, and "the discomfort he has long experienced in connexion with the College, hereby accept of the said "resignation.

"A correspondence containing statements affecting Dr. George's character, having been laid "before the Board, the Trustees decline to enter on the investigation of these charges on the "following grounds:

"*First*,—That there is no complainant to satisfy the requirements of the Charter.

" *Second*,—That there is no probability, from the nature of the allegations, of bringing the
" investigation of them to a decisive issue till long after Dr. George's connection with the College
" shall have ceased.

" *Third*,—That the Board of Trustees have no right, like that of a Church Court, to continue
" the enquiry after his resignation and acceptance thereof.

" *Fourth*,—That they are not the competent tribunal to deal with Dr. George's moral
" character apart from his connection with the College.—Carried."

Extracted from Minutes of proceedings.

(Signed) **W. IRELAND,**
Secretary to Trustees.

FACTS IN EXPLANATION OF THE FOREGOING DECISION.

1. Of twenty-one Trustees present, there was not one to rise and say I believe this man innocent.

2. There was not one to say, it is desirable to retain his services a single hour about the College ; but a deputation was sent to get his written resignation.

3. When that written resignation was given in, there was none to oppose its acceptance.

4. It was virtually a choice between resignation and investigation, and Dr. George chose the former.

5. There was not one to propose a retiring allowance for past *collegedle* services to the old grey-haired man, with *third wife* and infant children.

6. What other inference can be drawn from these premises, than that the Trustees regarded him as guilty, and that his own conscious guilt made him shrink from the consequences of investigation ?

7. If his resignation was to take effect at the close of the Session, why, unless guilty, give it at the very time when he knew if not given investigation must follow.

8. Nearly two months have elapsed since his resignation under plea of ill health, and yet he has not lost an hour's teaching ! ! ! Is his ill health like his resignation, prospective, to take place at the close of the Session ?

9. His other plea is discomfort in the College ; perhaps that discomfort is less now that his colleagues in the same faculty will neither associate with him, nor meet him in the discharge of business in the Senate.

EXHIBIT 2.

Referred to in the examination of Plaintiff at Kingston, 21st September, 1864.

THE NO-CONSCIENCE THEORY IN PRACTICE—A NEW AND STARTLING DISCOVERY BY THE MOST PROFOUND
OF MODERN PHILOSOPHERS.

CANTO I.

I sing of one so much admir'd and loved
That all who him adore not must be vile,
And black indeed the heart could entertain
An evil thought of one so great and pure !!
What though 'mong loyal hearts one traitor liv'd,
Could love far better than our gracious Queen
The President of the United States,
And drink before her honored name to his !!
Yet he has judgment rare, and never errs,
And is incapable of ought that's wrong !!
What tho' that same vile traitor having gain'd
The young and trusting heart and plighted troth
Of a fair girl, and having plighted faith
With her, could wed another in her stead !
He is incapable of falsehood !! Then
What grave excuse gave he for breaking faith !
A weighty one indeed !! 'Twas this, that she,
The other, had compelled him to the act.
Republican in practice, as in heart,
He came to dwell beneath the sheltering wing
Of his idea of a perfect rule.
A broken promise is a common thing—
What signify a loving woman's tears !!
He'll be a preacher in a far off land,
And speak to others of that constancy
And love which he so well exemplifies !!

CANTO II.

But all at once a change comes o'er his dream,
And rampant wrath is raging in his soul ;
He storms and wields his heavy stick apace,
And swears he'll leave a land so vile and rude,—
A Church so base as that could entertain
Such miscreants as could before his eyes
And on *his pulpit* write " *The Scottish Bear ! !*"
He leaves them in his wrath sublime, and comes,
O highly favor'd *Canada !* to thee.
What ! Can it be ? And will that mighty head

Seek shelter 'neath the rule it spurned before?
And will that voice of thunder deign to beg
To be admitted to the ancient fold
So late despised, so full of deadly sins?
Alas! frail human nature!—let us draw
The vail, and pass we on to other scenes.

CANTO III.

His troubles o'er, now will he rest in peace,
The quiet Pastor of a country flock?
What is there now to trouble the repose
Of his calm, tranquil soul and heavenly mind!
Alas for human hopes! again the storms
Arise, and wrath once more regains its sway
Within his saintly bosom, and disturbs
His soul, so that he quits his post and leaves
His *well beloved* flock to roam at will—
A prey to wolves much kinder than himself.
A while again he rests his weary wing
To teach divinest truths to erring man,
Himself a pattern of the truths he taught!
Well nigh he scatters all the Church that's there,
(For scarce a "back bone" of it then remain'd,
Excites dislike which never can be quelled;
And finally disgusted, once again
Returns to watch o'er his forsaken flock.

CANTO IV.

Ere while the loving partner of his bliss
Sought quiet in the grave and left behind,
As pledges of her love, three daughters fair
To bless the lot of their bereaved sire.
He now bethinks him of the days gone by—
He cannot be alone! The *generous* man
Will now repair the errors of the past,
And take the spurn'd one to *his loving* heart.
Oh foolish, trusting woman! oft deceived
By men in whom the vilest passions reign!!
So was't with her,—she came, young love yet lived,
And threw her rosy mantle o'er the past!
But she was chang'd, some youthful charms were gone.
And disappointment reigned within his heart.
A few short years of misery roll'd on,
And she, poor wretched, miserable thing,
Once more sets sail to seek her native home.
But oh! how changed! Where was the beaming eye?
The hope that bore her on? the youthful dream
Of love? All fled like mist, and she fled too,
To seek a shelter from her *loving bud.*

CANTO V.

The tale is long and sad—let's briefly end.
A pious woman once in Glasgow found,
Mid haunts of poverty and deep distress,
A wretched creature on a bed of straw.
Mov'd with strong pity in her woman's heart—
" Who is the wretched creature?" quick she asked.
One solitary friend replied, " She is
Wife of the Revd. —— in Canada."
Once more—no matter how they made it up—
He'd bring her to his *loving* heart again,
And she, weak thing, consented to return.
In *manly generosity* he sent the funds
To bring back his *beloved* wife once more,
And did it in a style became his rank—
A *steerage* passenger he brought her home.
Short was the bliss she sought, poor, foolish thing.
Not long her weary feet had pressed the soil
Of Canada, when once again alone,
She died *deserted*—in *starvation* died !
Left in this misery by him who swore
Before his God and fellow-men to love
And cherish her till death should them divide !

CANTO VI.

Once more the curtain raise, and speed we on.
Once more he leaves his *cherished* flock behind,
He'll be *Professor* now, and teach the young
Pure morals in his *great Philosophy !*
Meantime a brother and a sister come—
A youthful pair, from their far distant home,
Followed by blessings deep, and many a prayer,
To the same place where dwells our *hero great*.
(The brother, too, was a Professor there,)
Professing much, he seeks their quiet home.
With frank and honest, open hearts, they meet
Each kind advance. Oh ! little do they dream
That like a sneaking serpent vile he trails
Around their home, to rob it of its peace.
Ah ! little dream't that brother, when full soon
His sister too fled to her native land,
That yonder *aged villain's vicious wiles*
Had driven her from his side, a shattered thing,
To seek for peace and pardon in her home—
Her early home, where all had been so bright,
Where clouds of sin and sorrow never came.

CANTO VII.

The wheel of Time revolves a weary year,
He cannot be alone—the grey-haired man!!
Daughters grown up to womanhood will not
Suffice to be companions of his age.
Once more, a *third time*, wedlock's chains he tries,
And great had been the uproar and shout of fun
To greet his happy nuptials, but for one
Whose kindly heart and suasive voice and power
To stem the tide of ridicule, and stop
The nightly march and merry *char' ent!*
And well requited was his champion soon—
Grasping his hand, he told him he could ne'er
Forget his kindly act. And it was shown
How well it was remember'd and repaid,
Not long thereafter, when he turned his friend,
With wife and little ones, into the street,
Because, forsooth, he dared to write what was
The truth. Truth often gives one deep offence ;
And so it was with our *illustrious friend ;*
For not content with turning out of doors
He turned his benefactor from his class,
And called him, in his *mighty* gratitude,
A *fool*, a *medman*, and a *liar* too.

CANTO VIII.

But this was not enough—the *mighty man*
Waxed wroth, and persecution raged apace ;
For not content with having wreak'd his worst
Upon the poor, misguided sister, he
Rose up against her brother, and would fain
Have him expell'd from out the College walls.
The persecution raged from year to year
With unabated fury, till at length
The persecuted brother sought redress,
And that redress, though tardy, came at last—
Our hero stood condemned, a humbled man.
Not one of all were there—aye ev'n his *friends*—
But rose to say, he has been in the wrong ;
Yet he had sympathy—*poor injured* man !
Why was not this kind benefactor cast
Deep in the Lake, ere he had written truths
Unpleasant to our darling hero's ear ! ·
Why dared that unoffending pair to come
From their far home to tempt his evil heart!
Poor men ! they might have left him well alone,
If but each member of society,
Who ever dared presumptuously to cross
His blessed path, were swept into the sea.

CANTO IX.

His wiles defeated (for he surely sought
To drive by persecution from his post
The brother of the one so deeply wronged,)
He turned—the *fawning hypocrite!* and held
The eager hand extended to the man
Whose ruin he was seeking even then.
For well he knew, could he but cast a stain
Upon his name, and drive him from his post,
Should e'er the tale of his own sin be known,
He then might say, the brother too was bad—
Who can believe in aught that comes from them?

CANTO X.

Now all seem'd peace again, and Time sped on.
Momentous word! The great revealer Time!
Six years of mingled bliss and trial past
Since first the young Professor touched the shores
Of his Canadian home; he seeks again,
With tender longing and with joyous hopes,
The scenes endeared by boyhood's memories,—
With eager joy he greets each well-known friend,
His cup of happiness is almost full,
When oh! a fearful cloud o'erspreads the whole—
A secret guarded well for six long years,
(By one who fain had guarded it through life—
By one who pray'd with sad, deep earnestness,
That all the past might be a buried dream,)
Came to his ear to mar each happy thought,
A tale of villainy, of shame and grief.

CANTO XI.

Again he sought his far Canadian home,
Hot Impulse said, "Destroy the villain's life!"
But Grace replied, "Let Justice take her course;
Do thy stern duty, leave the rest with Him
Who says, "T'avenge is mine—I will repay,
If man should fail to mete that justice out,
Doubt not, it shall be meted on that day
When every heart's deep secrets are revealed."

CANTO XII.

But this was not enough, and censure came,
A weighty censure from some *pious lips*—
That he, the injured one, should dare to tell
The injury, or whisper aught of wrong
That jarr'd upon their pious ears, and made

Them feel their "*demi-g—d*" was but a man—
And worse—scarce man—the vilest of his kind.
Why could not he too act the *hypocrite*,
And kindly take t' villain's hand in his,
And meet him as a friend and smile on him
Who cast the first stain on *their* family name,
And robbed a sister's life of all its charms?
All this he should have done, and why? To spare
The cause of *true Religion*—"Oh my God!
What fearful mockery of thy Holy word!"
As if thy Truth—pure, perfect, undefiled,
Could need the aid of aught so vile and base!
Oh let them not be called *Thy* servants, who
Would screen the guilty and oppress the weak,
Who cry, "Peace, peace—conceal the *wrong*, that *truth*
And Righteousness may flourish in our land!"
Father of mercies, let thy truth prevail—
Let it be known, thy word can never fail;
And thou hast said—"First peace—then peaceable,"
Thy kingdom never, never, needs the aid
Of wrong, of falsehood, or of man's device.

CANTO XIII.

Once more we raise the vail, and only once.
A grave tribunal's met to judge the case—
But no! oh stop—he rather will resign
Than that they should investigate the truth.
What *shall* he do? Now quakes his craven heart—
Oh! say, "I'm sick! I'm dying! let it pass!!
Congestion of the brain"—*poor martyr'd man !!!*
The case is stopped, and all is peace again,
And he is gone, *poor man*, to his long home!

CANTO XIV.

No! not so fast—for once you're all astray,—
Amid his lucid teachings was one thought,
Most frequently expressed, which puzzled me,
He taught that *men possess no consciences*,
But that it is *instilled*, and taught to *grow*.
And now two questions rise within my mind—
The first—was ever one instilled in him?
If so, the difficulty soon is solv'd,
"*Congestion* of the *Conscience*" should have been
The plea, and *not* "*congestion* of the *brain*."
For since his dying resignation came,
He's never lost a single hour of Class,—
And still persists in being there, although
His colleagues do not deign to notice him.

26

CANTO XV.

And now one word ere yet we close the scene.
Why did our many have not stand up
And say, " Investigate—find out the truth—
I'll never quit my post until my name
Is stainless, and my character restor'd ?"
The conscious guilty heart forbade the words ! !
He wrote his condemnation. when he wrote
His cowardly resignation of his post ! !
And there were more than twenty men who met
To sit in judgment on his character.
Among the whole one was not found to rise
And say, " I think this man is innocent."
Nor yet to say, " Let us retain him here."
But unanimity prevailed for once,
" Accept his resignation—let him go,"
And moving pity bids me pause and weep
O'er his unmerited calamity ! ! !

CANTO XVI.

Now let us drop the curtain o'er the scene,
And leave the man, nigh three score years and ten,
To fondle in his joy his new-born babes.
Oh ! 'tis a lovely sight and oft admir'd,
To see an old man's children's children cling
Around his knees, and gently stroke his head
White with the snows of age ; but *fairer* still
And *far more natural* it is to see
That same old man with sturdy arms embrace
His own unconscious babe, whose infant gaze
Seems turned upon his wiry locks of grey ! ! !

———

Extracts from the Minutes of the Board of Trustees of Queen's College.

15th July, 1852.

Inter alia.

Resolved,—That the Committee of nomination previously appointed, be discharged and that the Committee of the Colonial Committee, with the Rev. Dr. Mathieson and the Rev. Dr. Cook, or whichever of them may be in Scotland, be requested and are hereby authorized to seek out and recommend for appointment by the Board Professors to fill the vacancies now existing in the College.

20th July, 1853.

Dr. Cook gave in a verbal report of his proceedings in Scotland in regard to the appointment of Professors ; laid on the table minutes of the General Assembly's Colonial Committee on that

105

subject, as also testimonials in favour of Mr. Weir, and Mr. Geddes, and further expressed, in strong terms, the favourable opinion entertained of the Rev. W. Milroy by Dr. Fleming, Professor of Moral Philosophy in the University of Glasgow.

Resolved,—That Dr. Cook be authorized to write to Professor Menzies in name of the Board, requesting him to nominate Mr. Weir or Mr. Geddes to the Classical Chair in this University, or failing them, such other person as he thinks qualified.

1st October, 1853.

Letters to the Chairman from the Rev. Dr. Cook and Hugh Allan, Esq., intimating that Mr. Weir had accepted the Classical Professorship in the College and would be in Kingston early in October, were read by the Secretary.

8th June, 1854.

Moved and seconded that the appointment of Professor Weir be approved of and confirmed from the period of his arrival in Kingston. The motion was carried.—Dr. McGill dissenting.

8th August, 1861.

A letter from the Rev. Dr. Leitch, dated 10 July, 1861, having been read, bringing under the notice of the Board certain contingencies in the event of a Union of the Churches, which might affect the permanency of his appointment, of which the following is an extract:—" That " the Queen's College engage to pay Dr. Leitch, as Principal of the College, a salary of six " hundred pounds, under the following conditions: 1st. That if the funds of the College " suffer any abatement so as to lead to a diminution of the salaries of the other existing " chairs in Arts and Theology, Dr. Leitch's salary may, at the pleasure of the Trustees, be " reduced to an extent not exceeding the proportion in which the salaries of these chairs, taken " as a whole, are reduced. 2nd. That in like manner should the funds of the College be aug- " mented, and the other salaries in Arts and Theology be increased, Dr. Leitch's salary shall be " increased in a proportion not less than the other salaries in Arts and Theology are, as a whole, " increased. 3rd. That in the event of Dr. Leitch being deprived of the status of a minis- " ter of the Church of Scotland, all payment to him by the College shall cease. 4th. " That if Dr. Leitch be removed from the office of Principal on any other ground than depriva- " tion of his status as a minister of the Church of Scotland, the College shall pay him a retiring " allowance of not less than two-thirds of his salary at the time of removal." The Board held that the permanency of Dr. Leitch's appointment cannot be called in question, but, in order to remove certain doubts on the point, which, it appears by his letter, have arisen in Dr. Leitch's mind, the Board unanimously agreed to adopt the following resolutions—on motion of the Rev. Dr. Urquhart, seconded by the Rev. Dr. Machar:—

1st. The Board agreed to the first two conditions stated in Dr. Leitch's letter, on the under- standing that the increase referred to in the second be from public sources, and not from fees.

2nd. The Board also agreed to the third condition.

3rd. With reference to the fourth condition the Board do not and cannot contemplate the occurrence of any such contingencies as Dr. Leitch seems to fear may arise in connexion with a project of union, but in the event of such a contingency in connexion therewith as would cause his removal from the office of Principal, the Board agreed to guarantee to Dr. Leitch the retiring allowance specified by him.

The chairman was requested to transmit to Dr. Leitch a certified extract of the foregoing resolution, with seal of College attached, accompanied with a letter from the chairman, a draft of which was submitted and approved.

9th November, 1859.

The Board having entire confidence in the judgment of Dr. Barclay and Mr. Morris (confirmed as it is by that of the Colonial Committee, and by many distinguished ministers of the Church of Scotland) as to the eminent qualifications of the Rev. Wm. Leitch, minister of Monimail, for the duties of Principal, did and hereby do appoint him Principal of Queen's College from and after the first day of June next.

10th November, 1859.

Inter alia.

The Board resumed consideration of the matter at issue between Professors George and Weir, and having cited these gentlemen before them, and ascertained from Professor George that his charge against Professor Weir, as the ground on which he had refrained from all intercourse with him, was his having countenanced the letter of Mr. Bostwick containing a misstatement of facts, and manifesting an animus unfavourable to the College, the members of the Board were unanimously of opinion that even on the supposition that Dr. George should succeed in proving all he alleged, he was not justified in the course he had pursued to Professor Weir, and which had produced, and was producing mischievous results to the College.

Dr. George then stated that if, as he understood, the course he had pursued was, in the opinion of the Board, likely to injure the College, and he was not required, as he also understood, to express any change of opinion, he was willing to give his hand to Professor Weir Whereupon Professor Weir making the like reservation of opinion, withdrew his letter of complaint, accepted the proffer and tendered his hand, which was accepted. The Trustees record their thankfulness that this painful matter has been satisfactorily arranged, and express their confident belief that the harmony of the College will not be again disturbed by any recurrence to this misunderstanding.

8th August, 1861.

The Secretary read a communication of date 10 July, 1861, from the Rev. Principal Leitch, relative to his office of Principal. After deliberating upon the subject the Board agreed to refer the Principal's letter to a committee composed of the following gentlemen: The Rev. Dr. Barclay, (Convener,) the Rev. Dr. Mathieson, the Rev. Duncan Morrison, George Malloch, and Mr. Paton. The committee to report to the Board at an adjourned meeting to be held this evening.

12th March, 1862.

The communication from Professor Weir, of date 14th March, 1862, having been read, referring to the action of the Board on 12th Dec., 1861, in the matter of Professor George, and requesting the Board to enter upon the investigation of the charges against Dr. George, and to regard him, Professor Weir, now as complainant, and giving reasons for taking this course; and also stating that he had received no intimation as to how Professor George's complaint against him had been disposed of by the Trustees, the Board unanimously agreed to the following deliverance thereon, viz.:

Considering that when the case, to which Professor Weir's letter refers, was formerly before the Board, he expressly declined to be, or to be regarded as, the formal accuser of Dr. George in the matter referred to; considering also that Dr. George had resigned his Professorship, said resignation to take effect at the close of the session 1861-62. Considering further the long and anxious deliberations then given by the Board to the case, and that in view of the great difficulty of satisfactorily dealing with the same by a regular formal proof, requiring the testimony of persons, some of whom were resident on the other side of the Atlantic, and to obtain which, would have involved lengthened delay, the Trustees came deliberately to the conclusion not to enter on the formal trial of the case, which, in the then existing circumstances, deemed likely to be protracted far beyond the period when Dr. George's resignation would take effect. Considering, moreover, that this latter difficulty exists with tenfold greater force at the present time when the close of the session of College is so near, and when Dr George will, in consequence of his resignation, be no longer amenable to the Trustees. Therefore, whilst feeling the awkwardness of the position in which Professor Weir places himself, as well as the Trustees, by his declared readiness, at this late period, to be the accuser in the case if it be revived, a position which he had formerly pointedly declined to occupy, the Board do not consider that it would be for the interest of the College, nor does it appear to them likely to serve any good purpose now to re-enter on the case which was regarded as disposed of already, so far as it could be disposed of then, by them, in the circumstances.

In reference to the inquiry made as to the complaint made by Dr. George against Professor Weir, the Board acted on the understanding that the complaint had been withdrawn.

The Secretary was instructed to send extract of the foregoing Minutes relating to his communication of 11th inst. to Professor Weir.

7th May, 1862.

A general adjourned meeting of the Board of Trustees was held to-day.

Present—The Hon. John Hamilton, Chairman ; the Principal, the Rev. Dr. Urquhart, Rev. Dr. Macher, Rev. Dr. Cook, Rev. Dr. Barclay, Rev. Dr. Williamson, Rev. Robert Burnet, Rev. Alexander Spence, Rev. John McMorine, Rev. D. Morrison, John Cameron, Alexander Logie Alexander McLean, John Paton, George Davidson.

Mr. Paton's letter of 23rd April, 1862, was again read, together with the complaint respecting the conduct of Professor Weir.

Moved by Mr. Cameron, seconded by Mr. Logie, and resolved,—That Professor Weir be called before the Board and the letter of Mr. Paton read to him, explaining, at the same time, the position Mr. Paton assumes in this case, viz. : that he, as a Trustee, has laid certain charges before the Board, and is prepared to prove them.

Professor Weir appeared, accompanied, at his request, and with the consent of the Board, by Dr. Lawson.

Mr. Paton's letter of 23rd April, 1862, and his charges against Professor Weir, were again read.

23rd April, 1862

A letter from John Paton Esq, of date 23rd April, 1862, was read, together with the complaint, referred to in said letter, respecting the conduct of Professor Weir, which complaint was laid upon the table, against the reception of which Rev. Mr. Burnet dissented.

The following is a copy of the letter :

Kingston, Canada, 23rd April, 1862.

To the Chairman of the Board of Trustees of Queen's College, Kingston.

Sir,—In accordance with the understanding at last meeting of the Board, I beg to submit a complaint respecting the conduct of Professor Weir, and to request that an inquiry may be instituted, as provided for by the Charter.

27

In discharging this painful duty, I avail myself the more readily of your suggestion that the application should be made to you officially, as it affords me an opportunity of explaining the position which I have thus deemed it my duty to assume at the request of several members of the Board, and also of stating the motives by which I am actuated.

My complaint is, that Professor Weir's conduct, during the last four months, has been improper, disrespectful to the Board, subversive of order and discipline, and greatly calculated to injure the youth of Queen's College, and the interests of the Institution. The case between Professor Weir and Dr. George was finally disposed of by the Board on the 12th December last, and it was my duty, as well as that of every individual connected with the institution to accept that decision as final. I beg, therefore, to explain that the complaint is entirely based upon what has taken place since the decision referred to, and that I disclaim all desire to re-open the above matter.

Most deeply interested in the welfare of Queen's College, I have been impressed with the belief that the conduct of Professor Weir complained of has been injurious to the Institution, and this belief has been most strongly corroborated by many of the Trustees. The minds of the youth attending College have been directed from their studies and otherwise injured by such conduct, order and discipline have been disturbed, and the peace of the Institution broken. It is indeed a painful duty to complain of a Professor as producing such results, and one from which, under other circumstances, I would shrink. The facts, however, having come within my own knowledge, in common with other members of the Board, and a written complaint being deemed necessary, I feel that I should be unfaithful to my duty as a Trustee did I not act upon the advice of those members of the Board to whom those facts were communicated, and thus formally submit a complaint respecting the conduct of Professor Weir, in his official relation to the College, and as having been unmindful of his solemn duty to promote, by every means in his power, the moral and educational advancement of the students, together with the order, discipline and welfare of the Institution in which he holds an important office. As a member of the Board, I am prepared to assist in investigating and duly proving impropriety of conduct as complained of in the accompanying document.

I am, Sir,

Your obedient servant,

(Signed),   JOHN PATON.

See note Exhibit S, referred to in the evidence of John Cook.

8th May, 1862.

The Board having duly considered the various charges in the complaint against Professor Weir, in connection with the evidence in support of the same, are of opinion that Professor Weir has, in some instances, allowed personal feeling to prevail over the regard which it became him to have for College discipline, and, although in his peculiar circumstances, and in view of the party feeling which seems to have existed amongst the students, there is much to extenuate such indiscretion, yet the Board feel bound to condemn it, and to caution Professor Weir against making the proceedings and decisions of the College authorities the subject of conversation with students, either in their class-rooms or elsewhere. At the same time, the Board, in giving this caution, think it only fair to bear their willing testimony to the diligence, fidelity, ability and success with which Professor Weir has conducted the Classical Department during his connexion with this University.

26th January, 1863.

The Board entered upon the consideration of the draft Statutes, Rules and Ordinances for the government of the College, which were read and considered *seriatim*, and after lengthy discussion and mature deliberation, were passed and adopted for the government of this Institution. The Secretary was instructed to file a copy of the Statutes, duly certified by the Chairman.

Moved by Rev. D. Morrison, seconded by Mr. Paton, and *Resolved*,—That the Secretary be instructed to intimate to Professor Weir, that the Trustees regard the holding of the situation of Local Superintendent of Education as, in his case, interfering with the full discharge of the duties of his chair, and are of opinion that it should cease after the expiration of the present year.

2nd December, 1863.

The Minutes of meeting of the Board of 17th June last, and of adjournments of 15th July, 19th August, 16th September, 1st October, and 4th November last, were read and approved. The Minutes of general meeting of Trustees of 1st and 2nd October last, and of the Executive Committee of 10th November last, were also read and approved.

The Rev. Dr. Williamson, from Committee to whom the letter of J. W. Cook, Esq., to the Treasurer, relative to a deduction in the annual allowance to the College from the Temporalities Board was referred, submitted a statement upon the subject, which, having been read, was unanimously approved, and is as follows :

The Board heard read a communication to the Treasurer, of date 30th June, 1863, from J. W. Cook, Esq., Secretary-Treasurer to the Temporalities Board, informing the Trustees that, in consequence of the induction of the Rev. Dr. George into a pastoral charge, and a claim having been made by him, as a commuting Minister, for £112 10s. annually, the Temporalities Board had thought it right to retain the sum of £150 from the College allowance for the last half-year, till the legality of his demand was decided, said sum retained being the proportion of an allowance of £112 10s. per annum, from the time of Dr. George's induction.

Whereupon the Board unanimously resolved to make the following representation to the Temporalities Board, which will at once show that any such claim on the part of Dr. George cannot affect the amount to be paid annually to the College from the Temporalities Board.

At the time of the commutation, in 1855, a letter addressed " To the Rev. Professor George and the other Professors in Queen's College," was received from Hugh Allan, Esq., a member of the Committee appointed by the Synod to negotiate with the Government, and the Secretary of that Committee, after stating generally that the terms of the arrangement had been settled with the Government, that document proceeds as follows :

" One pleasing feature of the bargain is *the securing to Queen's College of £500 a year in perpetuity ;* this was done with the consent of the Government, by putting the £500 paid to the College by the Commissioners of the Reserves Fund, " *an* allowance of £125 to each of the four Professors, and commuting with them for that sum."

" Please let each execute these papers as directed in the circular letter, before witnesses, and make affidavit as to age, and return them to me by mail as early as possible."

It is ended in a postscript :

" If anything was to happen the College, the annuity would be paid to the Professors as individuals. It thus appears that the object of the arrangement effected with the Government was *to secure to Queen's College £500 annually in perpetuity,* and with this view Dr. George, as a Professor, as well as his colleagues, signed the necessary documents and made the necessary affidavits. So long as he remained connected with the College, he received his share of the annual allowance which it received, but when his connection with it ceased, his claim to that share ceased also, just as the claim of Professor Mowat, as a Minister in the cure of souls, to the £112 10s. ceased when he resigned his pastoral charge, and became a Professor in the University, by whom he has since been paid. And the salary of Professor Mowat being paid by the Board of Trustees, the sum of £112 10s. annually, which he would otherwise have received from the general fund, has been left for a number of years at the disposal of the Temporalities Board for the maintenance of Ministers in the pastoral charges of our church.

That this is the simple view of the case is further shown by the By-Laws of the Temporalities Board, which were submitted to a numerously attended meeting of Synod in 1860, and after full and lengthened consideration received the sanction of the Synod. The 13th section of these By-Laws is as follows. (Appendix to minutes of Synod, 1860, page 65.) " it is the duty of the Chairman and Secretary-Treasurer, on receiving from Presbytery clerk's lists of ministers of their respective Presbyteries, with the dates of their ordination or induction, to pay to the Ministers who commuted £112 10s. per annum, to the ministers on the roll of the Synod at the time of the secularization of the Clergy Reserves, but who were not allowed to commute, £ 90 per annum, and to all others, until such time as the Board shall otherwise determine, a minimum stipend of £50 a year, the whole in half-yearly payments, *and also £500 a year to the Treasurer for the time being of Queen's College, to be employed as heretofore in the payment of Professors, being ministers of the Church.*"

That the clause of this section relative to the allowance to Queen's College was deliberately passed the following extract from the minutes of the proceedings of the same Synod (page 35,) shows. " It was moved by W. Snodgrass, seconded by John McMurchy, that instead of the words £500 a year to the Treasurer for the time being of Queen's College, to be employed as heretofore in the payment of Professors being ministers of the Church, the words " That Professors of the Faculties of Arts and Theology in Queen's College, being Ministers, shall rank as beneficiaries on the Temporalities fund according, as they may belong to one or other of the several classes of ministers provided for by the By-Laws and former resolutions of Synod on the subject," which motion was lost by a vote of 43 to 6.

In short the Board of Trustees feel assured that the arrangement made with the consent of the Government by the original committee by whom the commutation settlement was effected, and by the By-Laws of the Temporalities Board, sanctioned by the Synod, is simply this, that Queen's College should receive in perpetuity £500 a year, and that therefore it is the duty of the Chairman and Secretary-Treasurer to pay " £500 a year to the Treasurer, for the time being, of Queen's College to be employed as heretofore in the payment of Professors being ministers of the Church."

The Chairman was requested to forward to the Secretary-Treasurer of the Temporalities Board, J. W. Cook, Esq., extract of the above statement, with a letter soliciting the manager of the Board to take a favourable view of the case.

9th February, 1864.

A general adjourned meeting of the Trustees was held this evening.

Present : The Hon. John Hamilton, chairman, the Rev. Dr. Williamson, the Rev. Dr. Urquhart, the Rev. Dr. Mathieson, the Hon. Alex. Spence, the Rev. John McMorine, the Rev. George Bell, the Rev. Duncan Morrison, Judge Malloch, Judge Logie, Mr. Cameron, Mr. Morris, Mr. McLean, Mr. Allan, Mr. Neilson, Mr. Paton, Mr. Davidson, the Rev. W. M. Inglis.

10th February, 1864.

Moved by Hugh Allan, Esq., seconded by George Neilson, Esq., and Resolved,—That from facts which have come to the knowledge of the Trustees, and the present alarming state of the College, the Trustees deem it necessary, in the interest of the College, to remove Professor Weir from his offices of Professor of Classics and Secretary to the Senatus; and in the exercise of their power to remove at discretion, they hereby do remove him from these offices accordingly forthwith; and that the Treasurer do pay to him his salary in full to the end of the present session, and for six months thereafter in advance in lieu of notice, and that the Secretary be instructed to communicate this resolution to Mr. Weir.

A vote upon this Resolution having been called for and taken, the resolution was declared carried. The following is a record of the votes. Yeas—Rev. Dr. Mathieson, Rev. Alex. Spence, the Rev. Dr. Urquhart, the Rev. D. Morrison, Rev. George Bell, Messrs. Morris, Cameron, Neilson, Allan, Davidson, McLean, Paton, and Logie—13. Nays—Rev. Dr. Williamson, and Judge Malloch—2. The Rev. J. McMorine and the Rev. W. M. Inglis declined to vote.

Moved by Mr. Allan, seconded by Dr. Mathieson, as follows: The Trustees having, in the exercise of their power, owing to the alarming state of the College, removed Professor Weir from his position therein, entertain the hope that no further action on their part will be required to manifest to all parties their determination to maintain and exercise their power of government in the affairs of this University.

They trust, therefore, that in the future the Professors will do all in their power to maintain harmony amongst themselves, and exercise due discipline amongst the Students, and that the result may be that a proper *esprit de corps* may be raised amongst them, and that the College will so prosper as to make it to be regarded a privilege on the part of the members of our church and the public to send their sons to the College, and that a copy of this resolution be sent to each of the Faculties of the College, and a copy affixed to the notice board. Carried.

31st May, 1864.

Moved by Mr. Allan, seconded by Mr. Paton, and resolved—That the minutes of proceedings at the meetings of the Board held on the 9th and 10th February, 1864, be now read, which having been done—

It was moved by Mr. Allan, seconded by Mr. Neilson—That the proceedings of the Board of Trustees at its several meetings on the 9th and 10th days of February last, and all the particulars thereof, be and are hereby approved and confirmed, more especially as regards the removal of Professor Weir from his offices of Professor of Classics and Secretary to the Senatus of the College.

A vote having been taken on this motion, it was carried by a majority of eleven votes, as follows : Yeas—Rev. Mr. Inglis, Rev. Dr. Urquhart, Rev. Dr. Spence, Rev. Dr. Mathieson, J. Cameron, J. Paton, Alex. McLean, Rev. Dr. Barclay, Alex. Logie, Rev. George Bell, G. Davidson, G. Neilson, Rev. D. Morrison, Hugh Allan, and Alex. Morris—15. Nays—Rev. Dr. Cook, George Malloch, Edward Malloch, Rev. Dr. Williamson—4. The Rev. Mr. McMorine, and Mr. Thomson declined voting.

Judgment of the Chancellor.

Mr. V. C. Esten on the argument of the motion for Injunction has, I find, held the employment of the Plaintiff by Defendant was during good behaviour, in other words " *ad vitam aut*

28

subpœna." That the Court has jurisdiction and ought to interfere to protect him in the enjoyment of his office. These are the only two questions of law in the case, and I think I should hold that they having been disposed of by my learned brother, the Plaintiff is entitled to a decree, as it is admitted that in his tenure in office is such as the V. C. decides it to be, he has not been properly removed from office. I doubt very much the jurisdiction of the Court to interfere. The evidence before me in no way alters the character of the case as presented to Mr. V. C. Esten. The decree will be to restrain the Defendants from interfering with the exercise by the Plaintiff of his duties of office as Classical Master, from appointing any one in his place, and from withholding from him his salary until he be legally removed, with costs.

Decree dated 26th, 27th and 29th September, 1864.

This Cause coming on to be heard before this Court in the presence of Counsel for the Plaintiff and for the Defendants, the Reverend Alexander Mathieson, the Reverend Hugh Urquhart, the Reverend A. Spence, the Reverend D. Morrison, the Reverend George Bell, the Honorable John Hamilton, John Paton, George Davidson, George Neilson, John Cameron, Alexander McLean, Hugh Allan, Alexander Morris, Alexander Logie, the Reverend John Barclay, the Honourable Archibald McLean, the Reverend James C. Muir, Andrew Drummond, and Queen's College at Kingston, and Pro Confesso against the Defendants, the Reverend John Cook, the Reverend John McMorine, the Reverend W. M. Inglis, the Reverend James Williamson, John Thompson, John Greenshields, Edward Malloch and George Malloch. Upon opening of the matter, and upon hearing the evidence of witnesses and what was alleged by Counsel aforesaid—

This Court doth declare that the Plaintiff is entitled to hold and enjoy his office of Professor of Classical Literature in the University of Queen's College at Kingston until duly removed or suspended therefrom, and doth declare the resolutions of the tenth of February, 1864, and thirteenth of May, 1864, in the pleadings mentioned, to be cancelled, and that the Defendants, the Trustees of Queen's College at Kingston, be restrained from in anywise interfering with or impeding the Plaintiff in the discharge and performance of the duties of his said office of Professor, and from withholding from him the salary and emoluments payable in respect thereof, and that a Writ of Injunction do issue accordingly. And this Court doth order all the defendants excepting the Reverend John Cook, the Reverend James C. Muir, the Reverend John Barclay, John Thompson, John Greenshields, Edward Malloch, Andrew Drummond, the Honourable Archibald McLean, George Malloch, the Reverend James Williamson, the Reverend John McMorine, and the Reverend William Maxwell Inglis do pay to the Plaintiff his costs of this suit.

(Signed,) A. GRANT,

Registrar.

Order for Rehearing, dated October the twenty-ninth, 1864.

Upon the application of Defendants (who answered Plaintiff's Bill), and upon hearing their petition for the rehearing of this cause and the Judge's fiat endorsed thereon, and the said Defendants having this day paid into Court to the credit of this cause, the sum of Forty Dollars by way of deposit, to secure the cost of such rehearing, and having signed an undertaking to pay such costs as may be awarded against them in respect of such rehearing, It is ordered that this cause be set down to be reheard before this Court next after the causes and matters already set down.

(Signed,) A. GRANT,

Registrar.

The judgment of V. C. SPRAGGE upon the Rehearing is reported.—*XI. Grant, page 383.*

Order on Rehearing, dated the 7th of March, 1865.

This cause coming on to be reheard before this Court, on the Petition of the Defendants other than The Rev. John Cook, The Rev. John McMorine, The Rev. William Maxwell Inglis, The Rev. James Williamson, John Thompson, John Greenshields, Edward Malloch, and George Malloch, on *Saturday,* the *tenth,* and *Wednesday,* the *fourteenth* days of December, in the presence of Counsel for the Plaintiff, and the Defendants other than the Defendants last named.

Upon opening and debate of the matter, and hearing read the Decree, dated the twenty-sixth, twenty-seventh, and twenty-eighth days of September last, and upon hearing what was alleged by Counsel aforesaid, this Court was pleased to direct that the said cause should stand over for judgment; and this cause having come on for judgment this day, *This Court doth order,* that the said Decree be varied, so far as the same directs that the Defendants, The Queen's College at Kingston, the corporation in the pleadings mentioned, do (with other Defendants) pay the Plaintiff's costs of this suit; and with this variation, *It is ordered,* that the said Decree be in all other respects affirmed: *And it is ordered,* that the sum of Ten Pounds deposited with the Registrar, on setting down the said Petition, be paid to the Plaintiff or his Solicitors. *And it is ordered,* that all of the Defendants above named, except the Rev. John Cook, The Rev. John McMorine, The Rev. William Maxwell Inglis, The Rev. James Williamson, John Thompson, John Greenshields, Edward Malloch, George Malloch, and Queen's College at Kingston, do pay to the Plaintiff his further costs, occasioned by the said Rehearing, beyond the said sum of Ten Pounds. And it is hereby referred to the Master of this Court to tax to the Plaintiff his costs, occasioned by the said Rehearing.

(Signed,)   A. GRANT,

                                          Registrar.

Petition on Appeal of all the Appellants.

To the Honorable the Judges of the Court of Chancery.

The petition of the above named Defendants, the Reverend Alexander Mathieson, the Reverend Hugh Urquhart, the Reverend Alexander Spence, the Reverend Duncan Morrison, the Reverend George Bell, the Honorable John Hamilton, John Paton, George Davidson, George Neilson, John Cameron, Alexander McLean, Hugh Allan, Alexander Morris, Alexander Logie, the Reverend James C. Muir, D. D.; the Reverend John Barclay, D. D., Andrew Drummond, and the Honourable Archibald McLean, sheweth:

1. That a decree was, on Tuesday, the Seventh day of March, one thousand eight hundred and sixty-five, pronounced by Her Majesty's Court of Chancery for Upper Canada, in the above cause, which said decree has been duly entered and enrolled.

2. That your petitioners hereby appeal from the said decree, and pray that the same may be reversed or varied, or that such other decree in the premises may be made as to your Honorable Court seems meet.

And your petitioners will ever pray, &c.

                                  S. H. STRONG,
                                  J. McLENNAN.

114

Petition on appeal of the Appellants other than Queen's College at Kingston.

To the Honorable the Judges of the Court of Chancery.

The petition of the above named Defendants, Queen's College at Kingston, the Reverend Alexander Mathieson, the Reverend Hugh Urquhart, the Reverend Alexander Spence, the Reverend Duncan Morrison, the Reverend George Bell, the Honorable John Hamilton, John Paton, George Davidson, John Cameron, Alexander McLean, Hugh Allan, Alexander Morris, Alexander Logie, the Reverend James C. Muir, D. D., the Reverend John Barclay, D. D., Andrew Drummond, and the Honorable Archibald McLean, showeth:

1. That a decree was, on Tuesday, the Seventh day of March, one thousand eight hundred and sixty-five, pronounced by Her Majesty's Court of Chancery, for Upper Canada, in the above cause, which said decree has been duly entered and enrolled.

2. That your petitioners hereby appeal from the said decree, and pray that the same may be reversed or varied, or that such other decree in the premises may be made as to your Honorable Court seems meet.

And your Petitioners will ever pray, &c.

M. C. CAMERON.
J. McLENNAN.

REASONS FOR APPEAL.

The Appellants, the Reverend Alexander Mathieson, the Reverend Hugh Urquhart, the Reverend Alexander Spence, the Reverend Duncan Morrison, the Reverend George Bell, the Honorable John Hamilton, John Paton, George Davidson, George Neilson, John Cameron, Alexander McLean, Hugh Allan, Alexander Morris, Alexander Logie, the Reverend James C. Muir, D. D., the Reverend John Barclay, D. D., Andrew Drummond, the Honorable Archibald McLean, and Queen's College at Kingston, submit that the decree appealed from should be reversed or varied, for the following among others reasons:

1. Because the Court of Chancery did not possess jurisdiction to grant the relief which it assumed by the Decree to give to the Plaintiff.

2. Because the jurisdiction to give the relief sought by the Bill is exclusively confined to the visitor or visitors of the University of Queen's College.

3. Because the Plaintiff's proper mode of redress for the supposed injury of which he complains was by an appeal to the Crown, Her Majesty the Queen being the visitor of the University.

4. Because the Trustees had a jurisdiction, final and conclusive, and free from all control of the ordinary Courts of Justice, in the matter of the removal of the Plaintiff from his office.

5. Because the Plaintiff's tenure of office was not during good behaviour, or "ad vitam aut culpam," but during pleasure only.

6. Because the relief sought by the Bill is, by reason of the personal and confidential character of the office of a Professor in the said University, beyond the scope of the jurisdiction of a Court of Equity.

7. Because the Decree in effect gives relief by way of a specific performance in a case where the remedy is not mutual, inasmuch as the Court of Chancery does not possess jurisdiction to compel the Plaintiff to perform the duties of the office of Professor.

(Signed,)   S. H. STRONG.

115

The Appellants, other than the above-named Defendants, Queen's College at Kingston, submit that the Decree appealed from should be reversed or varied, for the following, amongst other reasons :

1. Because the Decree ought not to have given costs against the members personally.

2. Because the Court of Chancery has no jurisdiction in the matter complained of in the Plaintiff's Bill.

3. Because the Trustees had power to do what is complained of in dismissing the Plaintiff, and if dismissal was wrongful, Plaintiff's remedy was by action at law only.

M. C. CAMERON.

Answer of Respondent, George Weir, to Appellant's reasons of appeal.

The Decree of the Court of Chancery should be affirmed, and this Appeal dismissed with costs :

1. Because the circumstances stated in the Pleadings, and appearing in evidence herein, gave the Court of Chancery jurisdiction to restrain the Appellants from interfering with the Respondent, George Weir, in the performance of his duties as Professor of Classical Literature in the University of Queen's College.

2. Because the action of the Appellants in endeavouring to remove the Respondent, Weir, from his said Professorship, without cause assigned, or complaint proved, was in violation of the powers and duties of the Trustees of Queen's College under their Royal Charter of Incorporation.

3. Because such action of the Appellants was not only illegal, but entered upon mala fide, and demanded the interference of the Court of Chancery.

4. Because the Appellants, as Trustees of the said Incorporation, are governed by the regulations of the Charter with reference to their powers and duties, and any attempted violation of such regulations it is the Province of the Court of Chancery to restrain.

5. Because the Respondent, Weir, was as well under the Provisions of the Royal Charter, as under the general principle of Law in that behalf, entitled to be notified of any grounds of complaint, and to be heard thereupon before he had been removed by the said Appellants.

6. Because the Trustees of Queen's College have no summary power of dismissal over the Professors of the said College.

7. Because the Statutes of the said Trustees which assume to confer such power on the said Trustees, are illegal, and contrary to the Royal Charter of the said College.

8. Because the Respondent, Weir, was not guilty of, or in any way answerable for the alleged difficulties in Queen's College, which was the ostensible reason for the summary proceedings of the Trustees, when they ordered his dismissal.

9. Because upon all or any of the grounds taken in the Court of Chancery, the Plaintiff was entitled to the Decree pronounced herein.

ADAM CROOKS,
Counsel for the Respondent, Weir.

29

www.ingramcontent.com/pod-product-compliance
Lightning Source LLC
Chambersburg PA
CBHW030833270326
41928CB00007B/1034